Jung and Christianity
The Challenge of Reconciliation

JUNG AND CHRISTIANITY

The Challenge of Reconciliation

WALLACE B. CLIFT

CROSSROAD • NEW YORK

1982
The Crossroad Publishing Company
575 Lexington Avenue, New York, NY 10022

Library of Congress Cataloging in Publication Data

Clift, Wallace B.
  Jung and Christianity.

  Includes bibliographical references.
    1. Psychology, Religious—History—20th century.
  2. Christianity—Psychology—History—20th century.
  3. Jung, C. G. (Carl Gustav), 1875–1961. I. Title.
  BL53.C58   248.2   81-17395
  ISBN 0-8245-0409-7   AACR2

Even the enlightened person remains
what he is, and is never more than his
own limited ego before the One who
dwells within him, whose form has no
knowable boundaries, who encompasses
him on all sides, fathomless as the
abysms of the earth and vast as the sky.

C. G. Jung

Behold, the dwelling of God is with men.
He will dwell with them, and they shall be his
people, and God himself will be with them.

Rev. 21:3

TO JEAN,
WHOSE MINISTRY
IS RECONCILIATION

CONTENTS

PREFACE

Late in his life, the Swiss psychotherapist, C. G. Jung, presented Christianity with a challenge. In the decade that remained before his death in 1961 at the age of nearly 86, he was largely ignored by both Protestants and Catholics. This was a source of pain to Jung, for as "a lover of the soul" (as he once called himself), he wanted the Church to take up its basic task, the *cura animarum*, the care of souls.

All his life Jung was interested in the spiritual life of the individual. As a psychologist and a psychotherapist, he understood his work to be that of a healer of the psyche. He spoke of the great religions of the world, which had ministered to the human psyche and provided guidelines for the development of the soul, as "the world's great psychotherapeutic symbol systems."

Nearly all his writing throughout his life concerned the problems that an individual encounters in the course of his or her psychic development and, ultimately, with the meaning to be found in life. "Man cannot stand a meaningless life," Jung said at the close of his BBC interview just two years before his death. It was religion that had traditionally supplied the framework for an individual's answer to the question of meaning. Yet the institutional religions of his day did not seem to be meeting this need. For many it was the old problem of Galileo: the Church's adopting and "freezing" for all time the scientific understanding of the world at a particular time in history. For Jung and most of the people who came to him for help the Church had ceased to perform the theological task of translating the truths of the tradition into the thought forms of its day.

For religion to be able to meet the needs of its day (to answer the question of meaning) it must be in accord with, and understandable in the language of, the scientific knowledge of the time. I think I can explain this best with an example.

In the fourth century, when the Church fathers felt the need to express the truths of the tradition in a summary statement, they used the Greek philosophical conceptions of the nature of reality that were accepted at the time. The Christian experience was one of being liberated, set free, saved, redeemed, etc. Only the creator-God could be responsible for the *new* creation that Christians experienced. And yet, this experience was known to have begun in the community only after the presence of Jesus was experienced after his crucifixion. One thing was clear in the early centuries of Christianity—the encounter, the experience itself, was centered on Jesus, and further, it could only be described as *divine* (of God). The reflections of the author of the fourth gospel, as well as those of St. Paul, had spelled this out in the very early days of the Christian community.

How could this be said, in a summary way, for the first Christian emperor? In the creed drawn up after the Council of Nicea in A.D. 325, the Church fathers expressed it with the classic formula, *homo ousios;* the man Jesus was "of the same substance" as the father-Creator. Ultimate reality was understood to consist of *substance, substance* being the customary English translation of the Greek philsophical term used to describe the ultimate inner essence of anything. Physicists in our day do not use the word *substance* to describe the building blocks of reality. They have even split the atom, once thought to be indivisible. Since Einstein, we understand that all matter is a form of energy. In the language of the twentieth century, with our current scientific understanding of ultimate reality, might we not say, in our attempt to put into words the experienced truth of the tradition, "being of the same energy"? Putting a description of an encounter with God into words is never really possible; all the great theologians and mystics have searched for ways of doing so, but all have failed. A description of the experience is still needed, however.

Part of the problem for people today in finding meaning in the religious traditions of the past lies with the forms of thought in which those traditions are expressed. It is not that they are no longer "true," but that they no longer communicate. Every preacher in Christendom has probably spent some time conjuring up the world of sheep and shepherd, and the loving personal care involved, and the world of kings and royalty, where an acclamation of "King of Kings and Lord of Lords" has some meaning.

All of this might seem quite obvious, but the obvious is still a problem. Bible teachers may be schooled in the *sitz-im-leben*, the life-situations, of the gospel stories, but then their teaching becomes an interesting historical exercise of imagining another world rather than encountering something affecting our souls in the here and now. It was with this problem in mind that Jung published a collection of his essays in 1933 under the title *Modern Man in Search of a Soul.*

It is, in part, with this problem in mind that I, as a parish minister, first began to read the writings of C. G. Jung and later spent two years studying and experiencing the process of Jungian analysis at the C. G. Jung Institute in Zurich, Switzerland, in 1964–66. In the years since then I have continued my efforts at the "translation job," first with further study at the University of Chicago Divinity School, and then with teaching in a university religious studies department. My experience with college students has been that they live very much in the "now." They are interested in what affects them here and now. They are also concerned with the problem of meaning—as long as meaning is something one can encounter and experience. Their failure to find it in their home churches or synagogues has led many of them to give the missionaries of Eastern religions a hearing. My task as a teacher of the psychology of religion has continued to be that of a theologian as I understand it—translating the truths in all religious traditions into the language of our day which is, for so many, psychology.

I also encounter a similar quest among the lay people in the parish church I attend. For many of these Christians, an encounter with the "living God" is a reality that has become a part of their daily lives. But how can they use their minds to understand the experience?

Many Christians are put off by psychology. It seems to them to dismiss the reality of their experience. Jung himself once pointed out that just because something was explained did not mean it was "explained away," although many people seemed to jump to that conclusion. On the other hand, many people who have found solace in Jung's psychology have felt Christianity to be at least one-sided and, in its institutional expression, quite unnecessary. Can these positions be reconciled?

My answer to this question is both "yes, in part" and "no, not entirely." However, the book suggests that a dialogue between the two—Jung and Christianity—can be constructive for both sides. In Part I, I state briefly the basic concepts of Jung's psychology. Part II presents the principal facets of Jung's psychology of religion. In Part III, I discuss questions that Jung's psychology raises, including the challenges it poses for Christianity in several areas. I also offer a critique of this psychology from the standpoint of Christian experience.

Finally, on behalf of Jung, I want to add a disclaimer for what, to some, may seem to be sexist language. As indicated already in this preface, Jung was fond of using the term "modern man." He used the term to refer to a person who had reached a certain level of consciousness—not just to refer to a person living at the present time. He did not (and I certainly do not) have any intention of suggesting that modern women have any less of a problem with meaninglessness or rootlessness—or with the language of religion—than modern men do. However, I cannot change Jung's term, although I have sought to limit my use of it to those occasions when I discuss Jung's comments on "modern man." One thing is clear: the fact that I feel the need to make this disclaimer says something about the state of the collective unconscious in our day. A "corrective" is forcing itself into consciousness. Jung, I think, would find that not only interesting, but a sign of hope!

PART I

Basic Concepts in Jung's Psychology

Chapter One

THE PASTOR OF SOULS

Did he or didn't he?—believe in God—is the first question asked about Jung by people who feel they know you well enough (and think you might know). Most people assume there is a yes or no answer to such an obvious question. Yet the ordinary believer in the church pew, as well as the ordinary skeptic in the academic chair of doubt, finds the attempt to get an answer (if he or she pursues it at all diligently beyond a superficial reply) frustrating, to say the least. Jung is seemingly as devious as his favorite whipping boy, the "theologian," is often felt to be.

In an excellent filmed interview, *Face to Face* (in which the interviewer asks all the questions you want to ask), done by the BBC about two years before Jung's death, John Freeman asked Jung the question—did he believe in God? Jung asked, "Now?" (having recounted earlier his Christian upbringing as the son of a Swiss Reform pastor). When Freeman indicated his question referred to his present beliefs, Jung replied, "Difficult to answer (pause); I don't need to believe, I know."

Jung always insisted that he was an empiricist. Later in the same BBC film, when the interviewer asked him whether he "believed" something, Jung replied that he could not just "believe" a thing. Either he knew something or he did not. If he was confronted with certain data, then he would form a hypothesis. If given sufficient reasons he would have to say something like, "We have to reckon with the possibility of so and so." So Jung must have meant by his earlier response in the film that he knew some-

3

thing, that he had data which made him feel fairly certain about his hypothesis. He did not need to rely on "belief." [1]

Jung was always interested in *experience*. He wrote, "Only that which acts upon me do I recognize as real and actual." [2] In Jung's view, if God had no effect on a person, then God might as well not exist. If God was simply absolute and beyond all human experience, then Jung was not interested. But if God was something to be experienced in the soul, then, Jung said, "at once I must concern myself with him, for then he can become important, even unpleasantly so, and can affect me in practical ways." [3]

Beliefs, religious beliefs especially, were interesting to Jung and he wrote quite a lot about them, but they were interesting to him as *psychic phenomenon*. The fact that people held such beliefs was of psychological interest to him. The fact that they held such beliefs was a fact that could be investigated. What were the dynamics at work in the psyche? This is the essence of Jung's concern with beliefs.

Jung often used the term "soul" instead of "psyche"—perhaps to call attention to the fact that he was speaking of our spiritual side, the side that seemed capable of making choices that moved beyond the influence of environmental conditioning and genetic inheritance. The late Harvard psychologist Gordon Allport once complained that much psychology in his day was "psychology without a soul." With Jung, you have a psychologist who is concerned with the soul—and with the soul's concerns.

To the casual reader Jung often seems to be reducing God to simply an aspect of the psyche, as, for example, when he makes use of the expression "autonomous psychic complex" to refer to influences on the psyche beyond the control of the ego. The reader, Jung said, who assumed that this meant that God was "nothing but a psychic complex" was a victim of the typically Western prejudice that depreciated everything psychic. Jung found the charge of reductionism of any kind particularly galling, as his approach to the psyche was so open-ended. He wrote, "The epithet 'psychologism' applies only to a fool who thinks he has his soul in his pocket."[4] Such an accusation should be leveled, Jung said, "only at an intellect that denies the genuine nature of the autonomous complex and seeks to explain it rationalistically as the consequence of known causes."[5] That the source or "cause" of such influences on the psyche was unknown (and unknowable, Jung concluded) was precisely why the traditional term, *God*, was appropriate with respect to it.

Jung took the position that as a psychologist he would speak only about matters affecting the psyche. He found that some of his patients, when they pursued the path of "individuation," encountered a symbol of totality that could only be compared to the religious experiences of mankind the world over and throughout history. Jung spoke of this as the "God-image" in man. It was like an imprint on the psyche, but as to the nature of the "imprinter" Jung felt he could only respond as Job did and place his hand over his mouth. That a transcendental reality did exist and that it affected the psyche, Jung was confident, but, as he wrote in one of his last major works, *Mysterium Coniunctionis*, "It is uncommonly difficult for our consciousness to construct intellectual models which would give a graphic description of the reality we have perceived."[6] Once again, in the same late work, Jung responded to the charge that he had put man at the center (at the expense of God). If he had, he said, he had good precedent. Man has a central place in both Buddhism and Christianity, the two great world religions. And further, Christianity says that God himself became man. So, Jung said, "No psychology in the world could vie with the dignity that God himself has accorded to him."[7] In other words, to put his defense in the classic response of an introvert, "I didn't do it; God did."

Jung said he got into the business of being a medical pastor of souls simply because there was no one else to do it. Medicine rediscovered the psyche when it found that, while physical medicine might relieve symptoms, only psychic methods would heal a neurosis. Ultimately, Jung said, a psychoneurosis must be understood as the suffering of a soul that has not discovered its meaning.

Jung was perhaps the first psychotherapist to focus on what has become widely recognized as *the* problem for individuals today—the problem of meaninglessness. It is, in traditional language, a religious problem. When, as the poet Yeats said, "the center no longer holds," we have the anxiety of meaninglessness. Such an anxiety is, as one contemporary theologian has said, "aroused by the loss of a spiritual center, of an answer, however symbolic and indirect, to the question of the meaning of existence."[8]

Jung himself so understood his psychology, that is, as dealing with the religious question. Repeatedly, he said, patients would complain to him of the lack of any meaning and purpose in their lives. If it were not for that problem, they often told him there would be no "trouble with nerves." Outer circumstances did not give life a meaning, Jung found. It did not matter whether his patient was rich or poor, had family and social position or not. Rather, it was much more, Jung said, a "question of his quite irrational need for what we call a spiritual life, and this he cannot obtain from universities, libraries, or even from churches."[9] That help could not be obtained from those quarters was Jung's own personal experience; this became evident from a reading of his posthumously published autobiography, *Memories, Dreams, Reflections*. Nevertheless, perhaps we should take Jung at his word when he says that he began to deal with the meaning of life only because, as a doctor and as a fellow human being, he could not stand apart behind his medical persona, but felt compelled to try to accompany his patients on their journeys of spiritual suffering. A doctor who recognized the nature of psychoneurosis might be reluctant to enter such a territory, but, Jung said, if he intended to help the patient, he had to help him find what he longed for. "The patient is looking for something that will take possession of him and give meaning and form to the confusion of his neurotic mind."[10]

Even though Jung concluded that healing was a religious problem in such cases, he undertook the task as a doctor, according to his own account, because for so many of the people who came to him there was no one else. For his patients, as for himself, the traditional spiritual guides and philosophers had been weighed in the balance and found wanting. He and his patients were interested only in guidance that stemmed from direct, personal experiences. What the universities, libraries, and churches had to offer was someone else's experience. In his own experience and that of many of his patients, Jung found the basis for a healing of the split in the psyche in "images of wholeness offered by the unconscious, which, independently of the conscious mind, rise up from the depths of our psychic nature."[11] These images of wholeness were direct, personal experiences, and therefore not to be doubted. They met the religious need of the psyche that longed for wholeness.

In Jung's thought, the healing experience is not something one can will or make happen. There is a kind of submission involved, even as there is in a religious conversion. Psychic wholeness and health involves a kind of dialogue between consciousness and the unconscious. When confronted with something strange rising up from the psychic depths, Jung said, the patient recognizes that it is beyond the reach of personal will. The ego can give up its futile willing and striving. It is nothing less than a revelation, to which the patient cannot but give attention. In religious language one might say that guidance has come from God. For his patients (most of whom had problems with religious language), Jung expressed himself in more modest terms by saying that the psyche has awakened to spontaneous activity. In the products of the unconscious (dreams, fantasies), which consciousness can observe, motifs appear, Jung said, whose source in consciousness cannot be demonstrated. Jung came to call these motifs *archetypes* (to be discussed in chapter 3).

While such experiences cannot be *made*, Jung said, "We can draw closer to them—that much lies within our human reach."[12] Jung warned, however, against calling any such ways of drawing nearer to living experience "methods." The very word, he said, had a deadening effect. And besides, he suggested, "The way to experience . . . is anything but a clever trick; it is rather a venture which requires us to commit ourselves with our whole being."[13]

Jung recognized that his patients came mostly from a very educated segment of society. He said, however, that it was only a matter of perhaps twenty years before the concerns of the university became the ideas discussed by the mass of people. Religious truths had become hollow for his patients. They no longer felt "redeemed" by the death of Christ. For some, Jung said, it was no longer possible to reconcile the scientific and the religious outlooks; for others, the tenets of Christianity had simply lost their authority, their psychological justification.[14] Belief could not be compelled.

Jung believed that the problem of meaning tended to come to the fore in what he called "the second half of life" (discussed in chapter 4). There were none of his patients who had reached that stage, Jung said, whose problem did not involve finding a religious outlook on life. They had fallen ill because they had lost what the living religions of every age had always provided. Furthermore, he said, they did not recover without regaining a religious outlook. But, Jung said, "This of course has nothing whatever to do with a particular creed or membership in a church."[15]

What *did* it involve, if not church membership? What did he mean by his enigmatic response, "I don't need to believe, I know"? What did he "know"? How can we "draw closer" to those experiences which cannot be *made*, but which *happen?* When is an experience a *religious* experience? What is the language of religion? Jung said that you could not take away a man's gods without giving him some others. What about the Christian Church? If you leave it, can you avoid building another institutional framework? These are some of the questions to which I will return after an overview of some basic concepts of Jung's psychology.

Chapter Two

PSYCHIC REALITY
AND PSYCHIC ENERGY

The psyche is no less real than the body in Jung's view, and the concept of *psychic reality* is perhaps the most fundamental tenet of his psychology. Jung felt that while it had not been recognized as such, the concept of psychic reality was the most important achievement of modern psychology. For that to be generally accepted could only be a matter of time. He concluded, "It must be accepted in the end, for it alone enables us to understand the manifestations of the psyche in all their variety and uniqueness."[1] Jung's emphasis on psychic reality is what enabled (or seduced—depending on your point of view) Jung's critics to charge him with introducing metaphysical concepts while purporting to deal with empirical facts.

Crucial to Jung's theories is his understanding that consciousness originates in the unconscious. The temptation is to identify the psyche with consciousness. Or, if not that, to think of the unconscious as a derivative or by-product of consciousness. The latter approach is suggested by the Freudian theory of repression. (Jung does not deny the existence of such "by-products," and indeed makes use of them in his theory of the personal unconscious, discussed in chapter 3. But he does think it is misleading to view consciousness as primary.) In Jung's thought, such approaches tend to detract from the reality of the unconscious. The figures of the unconscious must, Jung insisted, "be understood as real and effective factors."[2] There is no need, Jung said, to fear that one has

9

thereby fallen back into primitive demonology, as long as one understands what is meant by psychic reality. But it is necessary to acknowledge the unconscious figures as spontaneous agents, for otherwise "we become victims of a one-sided belief in the power of consciousness, leading finally to acute tension."[3] With the growing acceptance of the basic perspective of psychosomatic medicine, Jung's principle of psychic reality will perhaps find a more ready acceptance, despite its threatening implications to those who would prefer a more physically mechanistic view.

Jung suspected that the material and the psychic were simply two aspects of one reality. Their separation in the traditional understanding of an individual as consisting of mind and body may have been a device of reason for the purpose of achieving conscious discrimination. Consciousness, in Jung's view, involves a separation into parts, and thus enables us to choose one thing and not another. Responsibility for one's choices depends upon one's consciousness, as English criminal law recognized very early in its development. Jung suggested that our experience of mind and body as two separate entities was perhaps "an intellectually necessary separation of one and the same fact into two aspects, to which we then illegitimately attribute an independent existence."[4]

Jung's conclusion in this regard came partly from his collaboration with Wolfgang Pauli, who won the Nobel prize for physics in 1945 for his formulation of the "exclusion principle." In their jointly published essays entitled *The Interpretation of Nature and the Psyche*, Pauli concluded that the only acceptable point of view was one which, as he said, "recognized *both* sides of reality—the quantitative and the qualitative, the physical and the psychical—as compatible with each other, and can embrace them simultaneously."[5] In one of his last books Jung wrote, "Microphysics is feeling its way into the unknown side of matter, just as complex psychology is pushing forward into the unknown side of the psyche."[6] Similarities and remarkable analogies were to be found between the two lines of investigation. If such a trend continued,

Jung said, the hypothesis that they were investigating the same thing would certainly gain in probability. With the limitations of our powers of thought and language, Jung saw little or no hope of our ever being able to grasp the nature of unitary Being, but he said, "This much we do know beyond all doubt, that empirical reality has a transcendental background."[7]

The question of psychic reality has received more recognition recently thanks to the widespread interest in "holistic medicine," as it has come to be called. If there is a psychic reality in the body which is unconscious and a psychic reality in the mind which is conscious, then, as one theologian has said, "the question which finally must be answered is: How are these two sides related to each other?"[8]

The key to Jung's psychological thought might be said to be the recognition of an inner world (psychic reality) and the extension of the concept of the soul (or psyche) beyond the ego (defined as the center of consciousness). Despite his medical background, Jung declined to make a purely materialistic reduction (as Freud had hoped to do). In the BBC filmed interview, Jung spoke of Freud's "purely personal approach" as one aspect of Freud's position that he could not accept. In his psychology, Jung wanted to take account of the cultural as well as the natural man. Both points of view had to be kept in mind, he said—both the spiritual and the biological.[9] Ira Progoff's book *The Social Significance of Jung's Psychology* called attention to this aspect of Jung's thought.

In the Tavistock lectures in London in 1935, when Jung was asked about the relationship of the psyche's experience of physical and nonphysical reality, he said, "The question whether the body or the mind is the predominating factor will always be answered according to temperamental differences."[10] Some people, simply by temperament, prefer a theory of the supremacy of the body, and so will conclude that mental processes are the results of body chemistry. Others will prefer to see the spirit as superior, with the body simply an appendix of the mind. Jung suggested that they are probably one reality and that we were simply unable to think how that could be. He drew a comparison with modern physics: "Look at the regrettable things which happen with light! Light behaves as if it were oscillations, and it also behaves as if it were corpuscles." [11]

Some of the implications of Jung's concept of psychic reality will become clearer when we examine the role of religion in his psychology. However, Jung's position is indicated rather clearly in a comment he made in a letter to a colleague very early in his investigations of the psyche: "A truth is a truth, when it works." [12] Repeatedly, Jung disclaimed any intention to speak about "metaphysics" (understood as speculative philosophy), but only about what he saw operative in the psyche. How well he succeeded is perhaps open to question. In her introduction to Jung's psychology, Jolande Jacobi wrote, "Whatever we know of the world or of our own being comes to us through the mediation of the psyche." [13] Upon this truth Jung would insist. As he said, " 'Physical' is not the only criterion of truth: there are also *psychic* truths which can neither be explained nor proved . . . in any physical way." [14]

When we turn to Jung's understanding of the dynamics of the psyche, we find he postulated a broad concept of *libido* as psychic energy—a kind of life-force not limited or restricted to one or two instincts to be found in the physical system. He viewed the psyche as a system regulating itself by virtue of a compensatory relationship existing between conscious and unconscious. As a self-regulating system, the psyche maintained its equilibrium just as the body did. Any process that went too far immediately and inevitably called forth compensations. For Jung, the theory of compensation was a basic law of psychic behavior. As he said, "Too little on one side results in too much on the other. Similarly, the relation between conscious and unconscious is compensatory." [15]

In Jung's view, consciousness is a differentiation of the opposites or other possibilities that are held together in the unconscious. Whenever there is movement toward one end of a polarity in consciousness, there is a buildup of energy around the other end in the unconscious. Dreams, for example, as expressions of the unconscious, can most often be understood as expressing a complementary or compensatory quality—that is, as telling the rest of the story. Jung's concept of the *shadow* and the contrasexual, as we will see, also stem from this viewpoint.

Jung's understanding of psychic energy is also a necessary predicate for his theory of types (discussed in the next chapter). The types are not static positions, but a dynamic interaction of polaristic psychic patterns of behavior and adjustment, in which any one-sidedness is complemented by its opposite.

Symbols are channelizers of psychic energy. They have their numinous quality because of their grounding in the unconscious and their power to channel the energy flow between consciousness and the unconscious.[16] Jung said, "The psychological mechanism that transforms energy is the symbol. I mean by this a real symbol and not a sign."[17] (This distinction is discussed further in chapter 7.) For Jung, a symbol is not to be regarded as merely standing for something else. Unlike a sign, a symbol *participates* in the reality to which it points. For Jung, it is this *participative* quality of a symbol that unites consciousness with an unconscious content.

Jung believed there was a general movement in the psyche toward wholeness, toward a balance. He sometimes spoke of this with an analogy to the energic principles of equalization and entropy, and his understanding here is not unlike Freud's postulating of a "death instinct" (*Beyond the Pleasure Principle*). When there was no longer a flow of psychic energy, when the tension of opposites had been resolved—this, for Jung, would mean life coming to a stop. This is true only in theory, as such a "task" is never accomplished during one's physical life. In the movement toward wholeness there are repeated resolutions, which, in turn, lead on to another experience of the tension of opposites—perhaps at a "higher" level, that is, more open to consciousness. Jung said that his energic viewpoint had long been a familiar way of looking at things. "Everyone speaks of the 'storms of youth' which yield to the 'tranquility of age.' We speak, too, of a 'confirmed belief' after 'battling with doubts,' " he said. [18]

Consciousness involves differentiation. Coming to terms with one side of the differentiation takes place during the "first half" of life. Coming to terms with the other side is the task of the "second half" of life, as we will see in chapter 4. This course of development Jung called "the path of individuation," and his colleague Jolande Jacobi said it could rightly be thought of as a *Heilsweg*, in the twofold sense of the German word: a way of healing and a way of salvation. [19] In this process of development, Jung found that for many of his patients symbols of wholeness would "arise," would come from the unconscious, and then provide a center of orientation or direction for their lives. He compared this to the role of symbols in the various religions, which he felt were no longer viable paths for most people today. Jung found that many of these "natural symbols" produced by the unconscious were in the form of circles and squares. In his comparative study of the world's great religions he found that such symbols were characteristic of most paths of salvation. He used the term *mandala* (borrowed from Buddhism) to refer to such ordered patterns of meaning. Thus, the imagination (understood as a response to images arising from the unconscious) is the key means by which the psyche moves toward wholeness.

Jung thought of himself as a dynamic psychologist; each part of the psyche he understood as being related to other parts dynamically through the flow of psychic energy. Because of the key role of the imagination and of symbols on the psyche, Jung was necessarily interested in the way religious symbols operated on the psyche. Of the individuation process he said, "The symbols used by the unconscious to this end are the same as those which mankind has always used to express wholeness, completeness, and perfection."[20] For a further elaboration of Jung's understanding of how psychic energy functions, we may turn to other facets of his psychology.

Chapter Three

THE STRUCTURE OF THE PSYCHE

In Jung's view of the structure of the psyche, there is consciousness and unconsciousness. One of his principle concerns was to develop ways of exploring the latter. Only products of the unconscious could be studied, he said, for "the unconscious is just unconscious. . . . We can only deal with the conscious products which we suppose have originated in the field called the unconscious."[1] Obviously the approach to the unconscious must necessarily be through consciousness.

The *ego*, in Jung's definition, is the center of consciousness—of my awareness of myself as myself. Jung recognized a variety of ways in which the ego perceived and reacted to external reality. He believed these to be innate typical differences in temperament and suggested a system of psychological types. He postulated two attitude types and four function types.

In the *introvert* attitude type, psychic energy flows inward; this type is characterized by orientation in life through subjective psychic contents. In the *extravert* attitude type, psychic energy flows outward; the type is characterized by a concentration of interest on the external object. Introverts tend to have what might be called an "automatic no." At the moment of reaction to a given situation they tend to draw back a little and only later are able to react. Extraverts in a similar situation "come forward with an immediate reaction, apparently confident that their behavior is obviously right."[2] Contrary to popular understanding, the attitudinal type difference is not necessarily based on "how much one talks," but rather, on the direction of the flow of psychic energy.

The four functions Jung regarded as systems of orientation. *Sensation* tells you that something *is*. It is the sense function. *Thinking* tells you *what* a thing is. It gives a name to the thing. *Feeling* informs you of the *values* of things. It tells you what a thing is worth to you. *Intuition* "sees around corners," so to speak. It sees the *implication* of something with respect to the past or the future. It readily discerns what the possibilities are. You may get a "hunch," as Jung said about intuition.³ Feeling, however, is not to be confused with "hunches," as in "I feel it is going to rain," nor with the sense of touch. Rather, in Jung's usage, feeling is a subjective evaluation.

In Jung's theory, the four functions form two pairs of opposites. Thinking and feeling are opposites on what might be called the rational axis. Sensation and intuition are opposites on what might be called the perceptual axis. One function will tend to be the most developed in a person, and its opposite will be largely unconscious. That is to say, with respect to the "fourth function," the one in the unconscious, an individual will tend to be awkward in his or her functioning. All four functions are "available" to everyone, and, at times, circumstances will require each of them. However, Jung's point was that one or two will be better developed and that the individual will tend to make more use of the better developed functions—even in situations in which another would be more appropriate, or at least more commonly used by others.

The valuable thing about a typology, Jung said, "is the critical attempt to prevent oneself from taking one's own prejudices as the criterion of normality."⁴ Conflict among people is frequently caused by the difficulty they have in understanding or accepting any point of view other than their own. Realizing that there are differences in the approach one makes to data at least opens the door to the possibility of understanding. Jung wrote, "It is my conviction that a basis for the settlement of conflicting views would be found in the recognition of different types of attitude."⁵ Jung's study of types may prove to be the single most valuable legacy for counselors in the field of human relations—particularly for clergy involved in marital and family counseling.

The *persona* is another construct in Jung's psychology. It may be described as an adaptively organized image of oneself. Every individual needs a system of adaptation or way of meeting the world. Each profession tends to assume its own characteristic persona or way of accomplishing the adaptation. "Only," Jung said, "the danger is that they become identical with their personas—the professor with his textbook, the tenor with his voice."[6] The danger is to be unconscious of the persona: to think that what one has chosen to be is what one is. One must not confuse one's "role" with one's identity as a person. The persona is the "mask" presented to the world, to society at large, and normally, one would wear a different "mask" on different occasions. It is not a matter of being hypocritical, but of being responsive to the situation. One needs a flexible persona, not one "glued" to the face. The persona is a mediating compromise between individuality and the expectations of others.

In examining the products of the unconscious Jung made a distinction between the *personal unconscious* and the *collective unconscious*. The personal unconscious consists of forgotten, repressed, or subliminally perceived matter of every kind that can be related to the personal life experience of the individual. The collective unconscious consists of elements characteristic of the human species. Jung wrote, "The collective unconscious contains the whole spiritual heritage of mankind's evolution, born anew in the brain structure of every individual."[7] The conscious mind is something that develops in each person during his or her lifetime. It accomplishes the necessary adaptations and adjustments to the world. Aspects of life experience may be forgotten or repressed and become a part of the personal unconscious. The collective is not derivative. It rather "is the source of the instinctual forces of the psyche and of the forms or categories that regulate them, namely the archetypes."[8]

Jung's account of how he first came to move in the direction of the concept of the collective unconscious is interesting. As a young doctor in a clinic, he said, he was approached one day by a schizophrenic patient who had peculiar vision with respect to the sun. The patient kept pointing to the sun, describing what he saw. He wanted Jung to see it, and of course Jung could not. Jung said he should have just dismissed his patient's vision, but was unable to do so. It continued to bother him as being something more than "just crazy." A few years later he came upon a newly published translation of an ancient manuscript which recorded a liturgy of Mithraism (a religious competitor of Christianity in the Roman Empire). It contained a description of a whole series of images in the same order as that of his patient's vision. Jung said he had to ask himself, "How on earth is it possible that this fellow came into possession of that vision?"[9] Jung recounts this story of his experience with the schizophrenic patient in several places in his writings. It was not a proof of the theory for him, but it did suggest the area for his investigations. Freud also came to recognize in his later writings that not everything in the unconscious was the result of repression.[10] Freud referred to such contents as "archaic remnants."

Jung made use of the term *archetype* to refer to the contents of the collective unconscious. He regarded the archetypes as analogous to the instincts, except operating in the psyche instead of the body. The archetype is a pattern or a drama that is found in human experience. The particular way an archetype is experienced in an individual psyche will be peculiar to that person and will be drawn from his or her total experience, but the archetype itself is something universal. Some geneticists have wondered if there might even be a physical basis for Jung's theories about archetypes. Perhaps the new field of inquiry called sociobiology will have something to contribute to this question. Jung would probably not be surprised at such a development, for his overall view was one, as we have seen, which emphasized the close relationship of the physical and the psychic, though in his scientific work he did not seek to account for their interrelationship. He was content to focus his investigations on psychic reality.

One of Jung's earliest investigations of the unconscious was his word-association experiments, which he conducted prior to his meeting with Freud. These led him to the discovery of what he called a *complex* in the psyche. In the beginning, Jung's theories about the psyche were called "complex psychology," and this term occurs in some of his writings. Eventually, he adopted the term "analytical psychology" to distinguish his theories from Freud's psychoanalysis. In recent years, the term "archetypal psychology" has sometimes been used with reference to Jung's personality theory.

A *complex* is a cluster of associations and associated meanings around a nucleus of meaning that has a great deal of "feeling tone" or a numinous quality to it. Many of these complexes that were split off from consciousness resulted from repressions for one reason or another (in accordance with Freud's theories about the origin of the unconscious), but some, Jung believed, had never been in consciousness before. Jung later related his discussion of the *shadow* and the *anima/animus* (discussed below) to his early theories about the complex and adopted the term *archetype* as a means of discussing the contents of such complexes. He wrote, "Complexes are autonomous groups of associations that have a tendency to move by themselves, to live their own life apart from our intentions."[11] In Jung's view, complexes might be described as fragmentary personalities. In fact, he spoke of the ego itself as "a sort of complex."[12]

In the course of the maturation process, which Jung called the path of *individuation*, there are a number of "steps" or encounters that can be discerned. One of the first psychic entities usually encountered in an investigation of the unconscious is what Jung called the *shadow*. It is a composite of personal characteristics and potentialities of which the individual is unaware. Usually the shadow contains inferior characteristics and weaknesses that the ego's self-esteem will not permit it to recognize; however, it does not always have a wholly negative content. In many cases, positive potentialities of the personality may reside, unlived, in the shadow. As all unconscious contents are projected, the shadow may come to be experienced first in a *projection*. To "withdraw a projection" is to recognize that an unconscious quality of one's own has been attached (unconsciously) to an outer object (other than oneself). While the shadow is projected, the individual can, as one analyst has said, "hate and condemn freely the weakness and evil he sees in others, while maintaining his own sense of righteousness."[13]

Jung defined *projection* as an unconscious, automatic process whereby an unconscious content transferred itself to an object and seemed to belong to it. "The projection ceases," Jung said, "the moment it becomes conscious, that is to say when it is seen as belonging to the subject."[14] The problem of the shadow and its projection is encountered in collective psychology as well, and is frequently illustrated in discrimination against minority groups.

Jung postulated a complementary, contrasexual part of the psyche called the *anima* in man and the *animus* in woman. It is the image of the other sex that we carry within, both as individuals and as members of the species. The inner form of the animus or anima is encountered in dreams, fantasies, visions, and other expressions of the unconscious, and the outward form is encountered at times when we project a part or the whole of our unconscious psyche upon someone in our environment and fail to realize that this other person who confronts us is in a way our own inner self. Jung's colleague, Dr. Jolande Jacobi, called attention to the need to differentiate oneself from the anima or animus. Inability to do so results in the "moody man," who seems to be buffeted by emotions and dominated by "feminine" type behavior, or in the other sex, as she says, "the animus-possessed woman, opinionated and argumentative, the female know-it-all, who reacts in a masculine way and not instinctively."[15] Negative aspects of the anima or animus are more readily discerned than the positive ones, and they frequently are emphasized in the Jungian literature. In addition, it is often problems associated with a negative anima or animus that lead a person to enter analysis. However, it is an error to suppose that the anima or animus is therefore something negative. Just as the persona is a mediating function between the ego and the outer world, so the anima or animus is a mediating function between the ego and the inner world. They lead the way in one's spiritual development—just as Dante was led by Beatrice in his vision of ultimate truth. Thus the contrasexual psychic entity also serves a positive function, and plays an important role in the journey toward wholeness.

Other archetypal images are frequently encountered in the individuation process. Among these are the archetype of the great mother, the archetype of the spiritual father, the archetype of transformation, and what might be called the central archetype, which expresses psychic wholeness or totality: the archetype of the *self*.[16] The goal of the individuation process is to achieve a kind of "mid-point" of the personality, where, as Jung said, "the centre of the total personality no longer coincides with the ego, but with a point midway between the conscious and the unconscious."[17] Jung called this center the *self*. For him, the self was a psychological construct that served to express an unknowable essence that could not be grasped as such or defined, since it transcended human powers of comprehension. It could just as well be called the "God within us," Jung said.[18]

The idea of the self was for Jung a necessary construct that enabled him to discuss the actual experience of the ego. The ego (which Jung defined as the center of consciousness) is all that we do know. Yet, he said, "the individuated ego senses itself as the object of an unknown and supraordinate subject."[19] That was as far as psychology could go. The idea of the self was not something which allowed for scientific proof. Yet Jung felt that a construct was needed for psychology to depict the psychic processes that do occur empirically.

Jung said his critics were mistaken in accusing him of equating the self with God. "I am an empiricist and as such I can demonstrate empirically the existence of a totality supraordinate to consciousness," he insisted.[20] What you call it or what "causes" it is another matter.

Chapter Four

THE STAGES OF LIFE

Jung has sometimes been criticized for his lack of attention to developmental factors in his theory of personality. In the classical view of Sigmund Freud, of course, the adult is understood to be largely determined by the experiences of early childhood. Freud's adult "character types" were correlated with problems arising in the various stages of infantile sexuality that Freud believed he had identified. Without necessarily following Freud's sexuality theory, later psychologists have found most useful the suggestion that what happens in childhood is very influential in the shaping of the adult. The criticism that Jung paid no attention to developmental factors is justified only in the sense that Jung was not greatly interested in child psychology. His writings and therapy proposals focused on the development of the mature person.

The central concern and interest for Jung was what he called "the second half of life." [1] The question of the "meaning of life" was particularly oppressive for the people of his day, he felt. It was the problem his patients presented him with, and it was the area in which he thought he had a unique contribution to make to our understanding of the human psyche. He wrote, "The collective unconscious is a problem that seldom enters into practical work with children: their problem lies mainly in adapting themselves to their surrounding." [2]

The question of meaning in life tended to be answered, Jung concluded, as one moved toward wholeness, along what he called the path of individuation. Jung's concept of individuation involves becoming aware (to the extent possible) of all aspects of the psyche, integrating these, and thus becoming a person no longer "divided." Observing the integration process of the second half of life, Jung identified several "steps" or tasks that are encountered along the way. Two aspects of the unconscious invariably to be dealt with are the shadow and the anima/animus, as noted in the last chapter. In speaking of "steps" or "stages" in the path of individuation, it should be made clear that the process is a lifelong one. Deeper layers or other aspects of the shadow, for example, may be recognized at different times during one's life. In carrying out the process of dialogue with the unconscious, a way opens up for the centerpoint of the psyche no longer to be focused solely on the ego. When this happens new meaning in life appears.

It was Jung's theory that consciousness, beginning in earliest childhood, was a development out of the unconscious. Jung compared this to the development of mankind, which he understood to be a story of the gradual evolutionary development of consciousness. Jung felt that this gradual development of consciousness in a child was something that could be observed. In the beginning there is no organized center for the psychic processes that one can observe taking place in a child, nor is there the continuity so necessary for a conscious personality. Without continuity there is no memory; without memory there is no sense of identity. Only when the child begins to say "I" is there any perceptible continuity of consciousness. In between those experiences there are frequent periods of unconsciousness. Jung said, "One can actually see the conscious mind coming into existence through the gradual unification of fragments. This process continues throughout life."[3]

Child psychiatrists and psychologists working from a Jungian viewpoint have begun to develop some understanding of the differentiating period in childhood. Michael Fordham, a London psychiatrist, has suggested that there are stages of development in childhood implied in the Jungian system.[4] He sees the developmental process of early childhood, or rather, the "first half of life," as being, in a sense, a reversal of the path of individuation to be followed in the second half of life. There is a moving out from a global, undifferentiated state at birth, just as there is a movement toward a new center of wholeness in the second half of life. The child encounters the numinous figures (typically Mom and Dad) who are "more than themselves" in the encounter. This is analogous to the archetypes of the "wise old man" and the "great mother" and other archetypal figures usually encountered late in the individuation process. The child moves through awareness of sex differences and is taught by society to follow the patterns appropriate to his or her sex, just as later one reverses this, so to speak, in coming to terms with the contrasexual as animus or anima. The child moves on to what used to be called in the churches, the "age of discretion," the distinguishing of right and wrong (the development of Freud's superego), just as on the path of individuation there is the shadow to be dealt with. And finally, the persona, one of the first things to be examined, usually, in the individuation process, is one of the last things developed or "differentiated" (indeed, if it is) in the development of the child— the trying on of various roles offered by society. This correspondence between the tasks of the first half of life and that of the second half of life can be seen in the table that follows.

Jung did not focus primarily on development in childhood, as we have noted, but underlying his thought is the assumption of the general adaptive process of childhood, which he sometimes referred to as the task of adapting to the environment. The process of coming to consciousness meant seeing the possibility of choice. The awareness of choice and the possibility of making ever finer distinctions increases with increasing maturity. The task of adapting to the outer demands of life requires roughly the "first half of life." The view of the psyche as a self-regulating system meant that during the second half of life there would be, unless blocked, a natural movement toward reintegration, toward adapting to the inner demands of life.

In Jung's understanding, the path of individuation involved a

STAGES OF LIFE

The Morning of Life	*The Afternoon of Life*
adolescence, trying on different roles	persona, awareness of roles
distinguishing of right and wrong, "age of discretion"	coming to terms with the shadow
awareness of sex differences	integration of the contrasexual, anima/animus
"larger than life" figures, typically Mom and Dad	archetypes of "the wise old man" and "the great mother"
global undifferentiated state	new center of wholeness; the "self" has become the center

reintegration of the personality. It was a moving beyond the differentiation achieved in the early years, and was an attempt, in a sense, to return to the more unified state by a holding of opposites in tension. Jung did not think there could be a return to the original state (unconsciousness), but rather, it was a kind of return in an enriched state. Paul Ricoeur's discussion of the modern appropriation of symbols through a kind of "second naivete" is comparable.[5]

The development of the mature person as he or she moves through the path of individuation will be influenced at each stage by the resolution or development personally experienced in the first half of life. The patterns of the collective unconscious are given content, so to speak, by the personal history of the individual. But the pattern itself—or drama—into which the individual experience is poured comes from the whole history of human experience. The collective unconscious consists of earlier evolutionary stages of our conscious psyche. As Jung wrote, "Consciousness is phylogenetically and ontogenetically a secondary phenomenon."[6] The psychic system has a prehistory of millions of years, just as the human body shows traces of its earlier stages. Consciousness arose, in the history of mankind, from an animal-like state that seems to us unconscious. Jung thought that the same process of differentiation was repeated in every child. The psyche of the child, he said, was not, in its preconscious state, a *tabula rasa*. Rather, it was already preformed in a recognizably individual way. The foundations for later psychic development were already present, although, of course, subject to environmental influences.

Basic to Jung's understanding is a distinction between the "tasks" of the first half of life and the second half of life, as we have noted. The first half of life is devoted to getting established: acquiring the needed tools in school, finding a partner and making a home, and getting established in one's business or profession. Neuroses are, in Jung's view, improper displacements of psychic energy. The symptoms that neuroses tend to produce in the first half of life are frequently characterized by a hesitancy to enter into these pursuits in the outer world. But, on the other hand, when the attitudes appropriate to that period are carried over into the second half of life they then become inappropriate. Jung accounted for the problems so often associated with the middle years of life by the failure to make this shift in concerns and attitudes. The counsel appropriate at one stage in life is not appropriate at another stage. He found the difference in approach that was called for enough to justify speaking of a psychology of "life's morning" and a psychology of its "afternoon."

In general, a young person is engaged in striving toward concrete ends, and any neurosis that develops arises from his or her hesitation or shrinking back from that necessity. On the other hand, an older person is called upon to contract his or her forces and affirm what has been achieved. The neuroses of the latter,

Jung said, stem mainly from clinging to a youthful attitude that is now out of season. "What was a normal goal for the young man becomes a neurotic hindrance to the old," Jung said.[7]

In the latter half of life one has to come to terms with the inner world, just as one had to do with the outer world during the first half of life. Differentiation of the opposites, or making a choice, characterized the coming to consciousness during the first half of life; unification or reintegration is the task of the second half of life. What this entails is the problem of raising to consciousness "the opposite," or other possibility, buried in the unconscious. From this experience stems new power. Such an experience has long been described in our spiritual history as one of "rebirth" or renewal.

For both the first half of life and the second half of life there must be a "moving out" to a new position. If the psychic energy is tied up in other ways (neurosis), then the unfolding self-development of the psyche cannot proceed as it would otherwise do. Neuroses, Jung says, "are seeds that fail to sprout owing to the inclement conditions of inner and outer nature."[8]

The means by which the reintegration takes place is the establishment of a "dialogue" between the unconscious and consciousness. The ego must "submit" to some other direction than simply its own conscious willing and striving; some "listening" must be done. Just as symbols provide the "channels" for psychic energy, as we have noted, so are they the "bridge" between the unconscious and the ego. They are the necessary means by which the two are brought together. Symbols, as long as they continue to live as symbols (and have not become mere signs) maintain both aspects: they can be approached by consciousness but continue to participate in that to which they point, which remains unknown to us—which is to say, remains unconscious. About the manifold meaning of symbols, Jung wrote, "The discriminating intellect naturally keeps on trying to establish their singleness of meaning and thus misses the essential point."[9]

Jung's seemingly strange interest in medieval alchemy stemmed from the fact that he found the processes described by the alchemists to be analogous to the path of maturation human personality followed. He viewed the alchemists' work as a projection. At least some of the alchemists seemed to have been aware that it was human personality they were working on, though this is difficult to discern as the alchemists presupposed the ancient idea of "correspondence"—that what happened in the physical world corresponded to a situation in the spiritual world. One of Jung's last major works, *Mysterium Coniunctionis*, was devoted to an interpretation of the alchemical symbolism. He wrote, "We can see today that the entire alchemical procedure for uniting the opposites . . . could just as well represent the individuation process of a single individual."[10] The advantage provided by alchemy for Jung was that no single individual ever expresses the richness and scope of the alchemical symbolism.

Symbols are, as Jung said, the mechanism by which the psyche accomplished its self-regulation—the means by which there is a mediation between consciousness and the unconscious. Thus a focus on symbols "rising up from the unconscious" is the way "modern" men and women (for whom the "dogmatic symbols" no longer resonate) can move toward that reintegration of the psyche that characterized "wholeness" in Jung's view. We cannot return to the state of the primitive, who existed largely in the "dreaming world" anthropologists have described for us. But, Jung said, we too live by myth; in fact, we cannot live without it.[11] By "myth" Jung meant a story that gives meaning, value, and orientation to one's life. Attention to symbols through the imagination is the means for moving forward with life and for discovering one's own "story." For the contemporary person in the second half of life this requires a conscious process, for we have lost the ability to respond to symbols in any depth. Our problem is that symbols have become merely signs, one-dimensional in meaning.

The process of development through the stages of life is largely an automatic one, a natural process. Normally the process runs its course unconsciously, just as acorns become oak trees and children grow into adults. But if the movement toward wholeness is made consciously, then a balance between the opposites has to be found. Some way is needed by which the contents of the unconscious can also be held together in consciousness. Jung wrote, "As this is not possible through logic, one is dependent on *symbols* which make the irrational union of opposites possible." [12]

When this natural course of development is impeded, psychotherapy may be of help.

Chapter Five

THE PROCESS OF PSYCHOTHERAPY

Jung's psychotherapy is based on his conviction that we are governed as much by goals as by "causes." Jung agreed with Freud's understanding of unconscious motivation—his is a "depth" psychology also. However, Jung's understanding of unconscious motivations stemming from past causes in one's personal history combines with a view of the individual as open to the future. We develop from a "pull" as well as a "push." One might say that Jung recognized Adler's power drive, along with Freud's biological sex drive, and added to these a need for meaning or an organizing principle—a need that has also been identified by existentialist psychotherapists. Jung said that to understand an individual we had to know more than simply how the person came into being. Today is only half explained by yesterday. Rather, Jung wrote, "Life has also a tomorrow, and today is understood only when we can add to our knowledge of what was yesterday the beginnings of tomorrow."[1] This includes even pathological symptoms. Neuroses are only half understood when we uncover their sources, Jung said, whether in "infantile sexuality" (Freud) or in the infantile "urge to power" (Adler). Neuroses were, in Jung's view, also attempts to form a new synthesis of life. They were unsuccessful attempts, yet they did have a core of value and meaning. They could suggest something of the direction indicated for future development.

For many, Jungian analysis has meant not so much the treatment of troublesome symptoms as the exploration and development of an inner life. Some Jungian analysts specialize in the treatment of mental disorders, but probably the majority work with people with a "normal" psychology who simply want to promote their own psychological development. Jungian psychotherapy shares with other psychotherapeutic systems the goal of setting the patient free for the possibility of making choices consciously. In the course of "removing the roadblocks" or treating the symptoms that brought the patient into analysis, the patient may decide he or she wishes to continue analytical work, having been introduced to and having worked with Jung's concept of the psyche as a self-regulating system.

Jung's fundamental principle, as we noted above in the discussion of psychodynamics, is that the psyche is a system that regulates itself by virtue of a compensatory relationship existing between conscious and unconscious. While Jungian psychotherapy has much in common with any other psychotherapy, it is this particular understanding of the psyche as a self-regulating system that accounts for the main differences. It is this principle or concept that opens up the possibility of receiving some "direction" or "guidance" from the unconscious for the development of the person. We have also noted earlier that Jung's view of the development of personality involves movement from a global unity first to differentiation and then to reintegration. However, Jung does not think everyone will be able, or willing, to move toward reintegration—at least not self-consciously. For those for whom such a step seems indicated, this is an aspect for consideration in psychotherapy. Jung's double-pronged approach, encompassing both past and future, is evident in his handling of symbols: he tried to discern not only what a symbol said about the past, but also what course it suggested for future development.

In the first place, symbols are to be interpreted as to what they say about the past, their "push" on us, much as in Freudian interpretation, though without restriction to Freud's sexual "dogma." (Jung described in his memoirs how Freud had admonished him never to abandon the sexual theory. In fact, Freud told him, they "must make a dogma of it." [2])

Symbols also are to be held and lived with—thus enabling us to discern the "pull" in our lives, the direction open to us for our self-realization. Interpretations that are to lead to insight in Jungian therapy also involve this second aspect, that is, the creative possibilities of the future.

Before turning more specifically to Jung's techniques in therapy, it should be noted that Jung always stressed the unique individual character of each analysis and each individuation process. When it came to psychogenic disturbances, there were only individual illnesses, and therefore only an individual analysis was appropriate. Generalizations were far less possible than in the case of organic diseases. In a lecture rediscovered among his posthumous papers, Jung wrote, "It is just as impossible to describe the typical course of treatment as it is to make a specific diagnosis." [3]

Jung held that various "methods" (psychotherapeutic systems such as those of Freud or Adler—or his own) were appropriate when the pathological facts were in accord with the premises on which the method was based. Some people had sex problems, others power problems, and for some it was more a question of the fundamental meaning of life, and so on. Jung thought that Freud's and Adler's theories of neurosis were helpful when there was "something that must be destroyed, dissolved, or reduced, but capable only of harm when there is something to be built." [4]

It was also Jung's contention that the "healing factor" in any analysis was basically the doctor's own understanding of himself. [5] He had to be able to cope with his own psychic problems before he could help others. In Jung's understanding, therapy was a dialectical process in which the analyst participated as much as the patient. Perhaps half of every extensive analysis, Jung said, "consists in the doctor's examining himself, for only what he can put right in himself can he hope to put right in the patient." [6]

In a Jungian analysis, as with most therapeutic systems, the first step is a discussion of all significant life experiences that the patient can recall, and an examination of the current life situation. Only when the past and present have been explored as far as possible does the therapist turn his or her attention to the unconscious.

Jung regarded contact with the unconscious as the *sine qua non* of mental health and the mainstay for the individuation process, whether the individuation process followed a natural development or was aided by the analytical process of therapy. He believed that the impetus for development was already present in the unconscious of the psyche. In one of his earliest statements about the purpose of therapy, he said, "What direction the patient's life should take in the future is not ours to judge."[7] The task of the therapist was rather simply to remove any obstacles to the path of development and to help the patient get in touch with his or her own inner resources. The latter process involved enabling the patient to draw suitable conclusions. Once the therapist had assisted in clearing away the roadblocks with understanding and insight, then the natural flow of development would resume. Jung felt that his theory was firmly grounded in his experience with his patients. It was also his interpretation of his own life, as he revealed in his posthumously published autobiography.

Jung regarded this "connection with the roots," that is, with the unconscious, as the heart or essence of life and its meaning. Without that connection one experienced meaninglessness. Maintenance of this connection and attention to it was, according to Jung, the essence of religion and the source and meaning of life. His experience with the unconscious and its products coincided, he believed, with Rudolf Otto's descriptions of the numinous in *The Idea of the Holy*. Careful attention to this, to the unconscious, is what is called for in religion. In fact, Jung said, that was the original meaning of the word *religio*—a careful observation and taking account of the numinous.[8] To be free to enter into life fully one had to pay attention to the ground and source of energy for life, either by means of a living religious symbol system, or by means of an encounter with the symbols spontaneously rising up from the unconscious in one's own personal experience. Reason alone was not enough. Jung thought that reason, though it may be adequate in many normal situations, proves inadequate in many of the decisive issues of life. A symbol cannot be created by reason, for it has an essentially irrational aspect. Yet it was a symbol that was needed to establish the connection. It was disregard of the "irrational" and an overevaluation of the intellect—of reason—that accounted for the contemporary "Babylonian captivity." Jung sought to help us find our way back to "Jerusalem," so to speak. Perhaps he felt qualified to do so from his own experience, as he liked to quote the Greek saying, "Only the wounded physician heals." [9] When the way of reason, Jung said, "has become a *cul-de-sac*—which is its inevitable and constant tendency—then, from the side where one least expects it, the solution comes." [10]

The "royal road" to the unconscious for Jung, as for Freud, was dream interpretation. Jung regarded the dream as a description, in symbolic language, of the current psychic situation. He insisted that any dream had to be examined in the light of the current life experience of the dreamer. Rather than attempt to apply a theory, the therapist should ask patients what they thought, or felt, about their own dream-images. In general, Jung said, dreams point out to us areas about which we have a "wrong" conscious judgment. This compensatory quality of dreams is a principal key to Jung's approach to dreams. "Dreams," he said, "are the natural reaction of the self-regulating psychic system." [11]

Jung's understanding of a symbol, which we noted earlier, becomes especially important in dream interpretation. He regarded the symbol as something more than a representation of a meaning which, as Freud said, had been "censored." The particular representation had significance in itself: one image was chosen and not another, and this had meaning that needed to be explored. In Jung's view, a symbol is the best expression available for something whose meaning is still largely unknown.

Jung called his particular "method" of dream interpretation *amplification*, and it might be thought of as being rather "circular," as compared to the "linear" direction of the free-association method introduced by Freud. The approach is by association or analogy, but after each association is made there is a return to the original symbol. Jung regarded the personal context as very important— that is, the personal associations an individual might have with a symbol. He spoke of this as *personal amplification*. The patient is asked his or her associations for each item or figure in the dream. By "associations" are meant spontaneous feelings, thoughts, and memories that come to mind concerning any given item in the dream. All together these provide the personal context of the dream and may in themselves suggest a significant meaning of the dream.

Jung also spoke of *general amplification*, which is done by the psychotherapist, who provides collective, archetypal associations with elements in the dream, derived from parallel imagery in mythology, legend, folklore, and so on. For example, if a patient dreamed of a horse, the patient would be asked for all his or her personal associations, such as his or her first memory of seeing a horse, or riding a horse, etc. The general amplification, added by the analyst to those personal associations might include such items from mythology as the story of Pegasus or the central Asian religious practice of a horse sacrifice, etc. Jung believed that this general amplification by the therapist had an effect even beyond whatever clues it suggested as to the dream's meaning. Modern therapy, he felt, was largely unaware of the therapeutic importance of a diagnosis. However, Jung said, "In ancient medicine it was well known that the raising of the personal disease to a higher and more impersonal level had a curative effect."[12] Most of us have had at least a slight feeling of relief when the doctor told us that our strange malady had a name.

Jung also preferred to analyze *series* of dreams instead of just one dream. Dreams have a history. One can often discern a sequence. A dream should be recognized as "part of the psychic tissue that is continuous, for . . . we have no reason to think that there is any gap in the processes of nature."[13]

Other products of the unconscious, in addition to dreams, are given attention. Jung frequently asked his patients to draw, or paint, or engage in any other creative activity they felt like, on the theory that the hands or body sometimes reveal that of which the mind was not consciously aware. The same interpretation of symbols through personal associations and general amplification is applied to such material. The transference, too, is given attention in a Jungian analysis.

Jung had still another, probably unique, technique for analyzing the contents of the unconscious, which he called *active imagination*.[14] This method tends to be used in later stages of analysis and only when the analyst feels it is safe to suggest its use. There is the danger for those who are on the borderline of a psychotic break that unconscious contents will be activated which will overwhelm the conscious point of view. Jung said that active imagination is "not a plaything for children."[15]

The technique involves letting the imagination move as it will, rather than as the ego chooses. The images have a life of their own if we allow them. Consciousness is involved in choosing the point of beginning and in observing the development. One may choose a dream figure or other mental picture and then concentrate on it. If we do not interfere, the image begins to stir, to become enriched with details and to move and develop. Jung said that while we are likely to mistrust the development as our own invention, it is a mistake to do so, for we tend to overestimate the power of intention and will. In describing the technique Jung said that "when we are careful not to interrupt the natural flow of events, our unconscious will produce a series of images which make a complete story."[16]

The products of active imagination are analyzed in the same way as dreams and other products of the unconscious. This method permits, however, a question posed in a dream to be pursued in a kind of imaginative activity that is only partly "directed." A degree of "wholeness" becomes possible as this dialogue between the unconscious and consciousness is developed.

As Jung saw it, the modern individual, imprisoned within a *weltanschauung*—a "world view"—which knew nothing of the collective unconscious and the creative potential there present, was cut off from his or her roots, from the source of his or her being. A world in which all symbols had become lifeless and in which the symbolic language of dreams (even when given attention, as in Freudian psychoanalysis) were reduced to mere signs used by a "censor" to stand for something else in the personal unconscious—such a world was indeed a narrow prisonhouse in which the full possibilities of self-realization would likely be stifled. Jung believed that we have to have a center of meaning, some organizing principle for life. He spoke of the hunger for meaning: "You can take away a man's gods, but only to give him others in return." [17] We will place our trust in something. When there is nothing that "grabs" our allegiance is precisely when we are ill. About one patient whose life was literally "godless," Jung said, "And that, for him—though he did not realize it—meant a dire loss of hope and energy." [18] Jung's task as a therapist, as he saw it, was to restore the possibility of meaning in life for his patients: first, by helping them through insight to release as much of the psychic energy tied up in neuroses as possible; and secondly, to help them discover new channels for that psychic energy in the symbols that rise spontaneously from the unconscious once the roadblocks have been removed.

The title of one of Jung's most popular collection of essays, *Modern Man in Search of a Soul*, indicates Jung's understanding of our general predicament. "Soul" was the term Jung used for a "connection with the roots," that is, with the unconscious. The primitive's concern or fear of a "loss of soul" was precisely what contemporary individuals were experiencing. Jung sought to help his patients—those, at least, for whom the way seemed open—to reestablish the "connection." He tried to give his patients a broader perspective by directing their attention beyond mere outer reality to the products of the unconscious, while retaining a conscious point of view.

PART II

Jung's Contributions to the Psychology of Religion

Chapter Six

INDIVIDUATION AND THE PROBLEM OF OPPOSITES

Jung called the world religions the world's great psychotherapeutic symbol systems. He said that for all his patients in the second half of life their problem in the last resort was that of finding a religious outlook on life. They had lost what the living religions of every age gave their followers. Their recovery did not necessarily involve the acceptance of any traditional creed or church membership, but rather their response to symbols that point the way for integration of the personality. The symbol systems of the world religions were "psychotherapeutic" in that they offered the means for that reintegration of all parts of reality into a meaningful whole, one to which the individual psyche could be related. In the paths which they charted, the seeker could find a balance in life and a sense of oneness or wholeness. In all religions, movement down the path is understood as a task, as something to be accomplished. Exploration of that path and the multiple experiences of integration and achieving a balance lead to that goal cherished in all civilizations—except perhaps in our own—wisdom.

Wisdom is to be distinguished from mere knowledge. "Wisdom is never violent," Jung says, for "where wisdom reigns there is no conflict between thinking and feeling."[1] "Folk wisdom" has always rightly been chary of too much "book larnin." Yet ever since the Enlightenment, modern Western culture has been hell-bent in its emphasis on rationality. We are all aware of the fruits of this movement, with its many technological accomplishments, and are grateful for them. As Jung said, "Science is the tool of the Western mind, and with it one can open more doors than with bare hands."[2] Science is the way we think. The trouble is, Jung said, we tend to think that the understanding science conveys is the only kind there is.

Reason was quite literally enthroned in the Cathedral of Notre Dame at the time of the French Revolution, and she has been our lady on the pedestal, demanding chivalric service ever since. Protests against too much one-sidedness perhaps can be seen in the recent presence of "hippies" and "flower children" in our midst. But the emotional and feeling side of life is still looked on with suspicion in our culture.

Jung's analysis of our culture is comparable to his analysis of the psyche: too much one-sidedness results in an enantiodromia— a pendulum swing from one side to the other extreme. If the age of reason was not born in Germany, it was at least nourished there. Yet, it is in Germany that the most antirational movement of perhaps any time in history arose—Nazism. In Jung's theory, the principle of compensation runs throughout the whole of nature. Thus, any individual or collective psychic development tends to turn into its opposite if it passes beyond its optimum point. Before that critical turning point is reached, compensatory tendencies emanating from the unconscious do appear. However, they are repressed if consciousness persists in its course.[3]

All religions are, in Jung's view, attempts to heal the split which the human person feels in his or her psyche. The basic manifestation of the split is that between consciousness and the unconscious. Reason and rationality are the results of an emphasis on consciousness. Jung felt that the West had made a tremendous leap in the development of consciousness, primarily, perhaps, because of Christianity. In its beginnings, consciousness must have been a very precarious thing. One can still observe in relatively primitive societies the great fear of a loss of consciousness. Jung thought that one example of this concern over a loss of consciousness was to be found in the term "going berserk" in Germanic saga.[4] Even quite ordinary emotions may cause a considerable loss of consciousness. One of the things the institution of the Christian Church had done during the last two thousand years, Jung suggested, was to exercise a mediating and protective function against that danger.

Jung understood the world's religions as responding in a compensatory way to the cultural situation—in other words, helping to maintain the balance necessary for psychic wholeness. Thus, he spoke of the spiritual disorientation of the Roman world as being compensated for by the irruption of Christianity. But, he said, Christianity found it necessary to rationalize its doctrines in order to defend itself not only against attack by its enemies but from a flood of irrationality from its own adherents. Over the centuries, Jung said, this led "to that strange marriage of the originally irrational Christian message with human reason, which is so characteristic of the Western mentality."[5] In the end, reason gained the upper hand in the West and gave birth to an age of scientific technology that, in turn, left less and less room for the natural and irrational aspects of humanity. That was the basis for the inner opposition which Jung observed in the outer world today. In its competition with Marxist rationalism, Christianity, by a strange enantiodromia, Jung said, once again found itself to be the defender of the irrational, for despite "having fathered rationalism and intellectualism, it has not succumbed to them so far as to give up its belief in the rights of man."[6] Christianity's emphasis on the freedom of the individual meant, despite the rational claims for a "dictatorship of the proletariat," a recognition of the irrational principle.

Ambiguity is avoided by emphasizing one side at the expense of the other; this is the easy, and even necessary, path. Indeed, clarity of consciousness requires a separation of possibilities. But, Jung said, "Wisdom never forgets that all things have two sides."[7]

The split in the outer world is analogous to, if indeed not the result of, the split in the individual psyche. All experience of immediate reality is necessarily psychic in Jung's view, as we noted earlier. That is why primitives deal with spirits and magical influences on the same level as physical events; they have not separated original experience into its parts. Spirit and matter, for them, still interpenetrate each other. With the rise of consciousness in the long history of mankind, spirit and nature split apart. The West, Jung said, responded by temperament to a belief in matter. The effort to be "spiritual" was a problem. On the other hand, the East traditionally emphasized the spiritual, regarding matter a mere *illusion*, and so, to the West's horror, paid little attention to such material concerns as sanitation, or the draining of swamps for the prevention of disease. But, Jung said, there is only one reality—one earth, one humanity. What is needed is an advance in consciousness to the point where the human being can recognize that psychic reality still exists in its original oneness—"Where," as Jung said, "he no longer believes in the one part and denies the other, but recognizes both as constituent elements of one psyche."[8]

How to heal the split? The basic problem, in Jung's view, was one of achieving a reunion of the opposites on a "higher" conscious level. In order to achieve this goal, individuals would have to undertake the difficult task of withdrawing their projections— that is, making them conscious.

As we noted in chapter 3, Jung spoke of projection as an unconscious, automatic process which ceased the moment it became conscious. When a projection is present the pressure of traditional or conventional ideas usually takes the place of real experience and prevents it from becoming conscious. In such a case, one feels that one possesses a valid truth concerning the unknown; however, real knowledge of the experience becomes impossible. "The unconscious factor," Jung said, "must necessarily have been something that was incompatible with the conscious attitude."[9]

The political propaganda of mass movements has exploited the phenomenon of projection. The only defense against this kind of danger, Jung said, is recognition of the shadow. Such an integration of previously unrecognized components of the personality amounts to a widening of consciousness. Jung viewed Freud's efforts to bring the shadow to consciousness as an instinctual response on his part to the tendency of the general public to make projections. He was unable, however, to prevent the nationwide psychic epidemics that occurred in Europe. Freud did not recognize that a confrontation with the shadow side (not Freud's term) was not just a harmless affair that could be settled by reason. Jung wrote, "The shadow is the primitive who is still alive and active in civilized man, and our civilized reason means nothing to him." [10]

The *shadow* is, as we noted earlier, the name Jung gave to the "other side" of the personality. It is a composite of personal characteristics and potentialities of which the individual is unaware. Jung said that generally we are less good than we imagine ourselves to be—or even want to be. Everyone has a shadow, and the less we are aware of it the denser it is. We have a chance to correct an inferiority if we are conscious of it. The more our shadow is totally unconscious, the more we are subject to it bursting forth suddenly when we are not expecting it. Jung said that we carry our past with us—including all primitive or inferior desires and emotions. To free ourselves from that burden requires a tremendous effort. One must find a way for the conscious personality to live together with the shadow. Suppression of the shadow would be no more remedy than beheading would be for a headache. Jung wrote, "To destroy a man's morality does not help either, because it would kill his better self, without which even the shadow makes no sense." [11] Bringing together in a workable relationship consciousness and such contents of the unconscious is a major life task. It is what Jung meant by the term *individuation*.

If the shadow were obviously evil, it would be a different matter. The shadow includes what are simply childish or primitive qualities, which would otherwise enhance human existence, if it were not for the prohibitions of convention. Civilization has tended to detach us from our roots, and from earthiness in general.

In Jung's view, collectivities are mere accumulations of individuals. The problem of the whole is the sum of individual problems. And, the individual problems are solved only by a general change of attitude. As Jung said, "The change does not begin with propaganda and mass meetings, or with violence. It begins with a change in individuals." [12]

According to Jung, the split will have to be healed in the individual. The only contribution the individual can make to society is to withdraw his or her own projection. That is what we can do for each other. "Love thy neighbor as thyself," Jesus taught. Jung teaches that we must pay closer attention to this injunction. To love oneself is to accept oneself—"just as I am," which, as an old evangelical hymn suggests, is the way God accepts us. Then, having accepted ourselves, we can accept others, just as they are. Then we can truly withdraw our projections. One is reminded of Jesus' admonition, "Why do you see the speck that is in your brother's eye, but do not notice the log that is in your own eye?" (Matthew 7:3) Jung said that all gaps in our actual knowledge are filled out with projections. What is needed is the courage to withdraw all such projections, to be conscious of the shadow to the extent that one knows that whatever is wrong in the world is in oneself. To learn to deal with one's own shadow is to do something real for the world. Such a person, Jung said, "has succeeded in shouldering at least an infinitesimal part of the gigantic, unsolved social problems of our day." [13] Jung saw the task of individuation as a process continuing throughout life. As we continue to withdraw projections, we continue to recognize and accept aspects of ourselves that we had not seen before.

Jung's view of the development of the individual is relevant here. The first half of life is given over to differentiating and bringing into consciousness the problems of life that come to the fore at that time: the sex drive and the power drive, with which Freud's and Adler's psychologies dealt specifically. The second half of life then involves the task of reintegrating (recognizing as an aspect of the self) that which we had not chosen. Ira Progoff, a psychotherapist who acknowledges his indebtedness to Jung, has developed a technique for individuals to carry out this task of integration on their own (or in the presence of others) by writing a personal and private journal. One section of the journal calls for the individual to reflect, as Robert Frost once said, on all those "roads not taken" in the course of one's life. That too, Progoff suggests, is a part of "who we are." Learning "who we are" is perhaps another way of describing the task Jung is suggesting.

"Know thyself," Socrates taught, and in Jung's understanding this is a process that continues throughout life. As a life moves toward a close (the "second half," as Jung calls it), the urgency to proceed with this kind of understanding increases. An individual who neglects this task or turns away from it—refusing to undertake the inward journey of understanding—begins to behave awkwardly, or may be troubled with an illness that no medicine seems to cure. Instead of becoming acquainted with the "woman within," for example, (the anima, as Jung called it), a man may find himself divorcing his wife of many years and chasing after other women. That is the literalistic, materialistic distortion of his own messages from the unconscious. It is an ineffective way of dealing with the problem of opposites.

The union of opposites is the task of the process of individuation. It can be accomplished as a normal process of growth—running its course unconsciously. But if the process is made conscious, then one is dependent upon symbols as the means by which the irrational union of opposites can be accomplished. A confrontation of the unconscious by consciousness cannot be accomplished through logic.

Religions (the world's great psychotherapeutic symbol systems) can be viewed as "salvation schemas"—systems of healing, of reuniting. The ministry is, as St. Paul saw it, one of reconciliation. A salvation schema has three parts basically. There is a diagnosis of what is wrong, naming the problem. There is implied in that diagnosis, usually, a goal or solution. The middle part is how to get from one to the other. ("What must I do to be saved?" is the classic question.) Theologians have not often posed this question in our day, not to speak of suggesting an answer. The psychology of the unconscious may have something to teach Christianity about the task of reconciliation. If Jung is right, our reconciliation with God (God as experienced in the manifestations of the unconscious) opens the door to our reconciliation with each other and with nature. Perhaps the new interest in ecology in our century is itself a manifestation of the longing for the healing of the split.

Jung tells us that the union of opposites is only possible by means of symbols. In the next chapter we will take a further look at symbols. What are they? How can they perform this "task of tasks" that Jung has identified?

Chapter Seven

THE UNITING QUALITY
OF SYMBOLS

Our word *symbol* comes from two Greek words meaning "to throw together," and this is precisely what a symbol does. It bridges two realities, brings them together into a new unity. Symbols (when they are still symbols, and have not become signs) possess a numinous quality, as they "participate" in that which is unknowable directly. To be symbolic, a word or image must imply something more than its obvious and immediate meaning. It has an unconscious aspect of which one is never fully aware. As long as something is functioning as a symbol, a rational explanation or comprehensive definition is not possible. As Jung said, "As the mind explores the symbol it is led to ideas that lie beyond the grasp of reason."[1] Symbols are, in effect, the best representation for an unknown content.

In a sense, man could be defined as the animal with the capacity for symbols. When we think of symbols we usually think of visual pictures, but verbalization and language itself are aspects of man's symbolic functioning. Words, properly arranged and delivered, can bring tears to our eyes and elicit deep emotions. They can *effect a reality* for us into which we enter and participate.

The father of depth psychology, Sigmund Freud, was also aware of the extent to which symbols were grounded in reality. In *The Ego and the Id*, he observed that "thinking in pictures" was "only a very incomplete form of becoming conscious" and was much closer to unconscious processes than "thinking in words."[2] Further, he suggested that thinking in pictures was an earlier development not only for each individual, but also in the history of mankind. Freud, however, never developed his understanding of symbols beyond this observation. On the whole, dream symbols remained for him simply disguises for the repressed. As Jung wrote, "What Freud terms symbols are no more than *signs* for elementary instinctive processes."[3] In this distinction that Jung makes between signs and symbols, signs have only one meaning, whereas symbols move beyond that. As the late Harvard psychologist Gordon Allport once wrote, "Thinking creatively with symbols is something beyond responding to signals."[4]

In *Symbols of Transformation* (the book, published in 1912, that contributed to his break with Freud), Jung wrote, "Symbols are not allegories and not signs: they are images of contents which for the most part transcend consciousness."[5] It is important for us to realize, Jung said, that such contents are real, and that it is not only possible, but absolutely necessary for us to deal with them. In his next book, *Psychological Types*, Jung elaborated further on the distinction between symbols and signs. For example, Jung said, the insignia worn by railway officials simply identifies them as employees of the railway system. The "winged wheel" is not a symbol of the railway, but rather a sign, with one particular meaning. On the other hand, a symbol is pregnant with meaning. It is a living thing, which cannot be reduced to a single dimension, to one definition. As a living entity it is also capable of becoming dead, with only historical significance, once its meaning has been born out of it—that is, once an expression has been found that describes and defines what was the unconscious aspect of the symbol. We may still refer to it as a symbol because it had once functioned as such, but in Jung's language it has become a sign.[6]

Signs are often selected (or invented). They can be replaced. There is simply a convention that defines what they mean, as with mathematical symbols. Symbols, however, cannot be created so easily. They arise as a response to something in the collective unconscious. The shared history of a group may produce a symbol that not only represents, but actually makes present for the group something of their shared experience. We cannot "force" ourselves to be "grasped" emotionally—it simply happens. Thus it is impossible for us to create a *living* symbol—one that is pregnant with meaning—from known associations, for then it would contain no more than what we put into it. On the other hand, a conventional sign may grow into a symbol if it produces a response in a group at an unconscious level. Revolutionary movements often produce symbols because the movements themselves are responses to stirrings deep within the psyches of a number of people.

The *participative* quality of a symbol is its most distinctive feature—the ability to make present another reality, and to participate in that reality.[7] For example, an attack on the school mascot is, for loyal students and alumni, an attack on the worth and dignity of the school itself. Similarly, to mutilate or destroy a living religious symbol is blasphemy.

Jung makes a distinction between individual, personal symbols and social or collective symbols. In either case it is a natural and spontaneous product. In the case of a social symbol, it is not possible to take a thought arrived at by logical processes and then give it "symbolic form," Jung said—no matter how fantastic the trappings one may wrap around it. It is still a sign, with a particular meaning, and not a symbol that is reverberating with something as yet unknown. It is, however, possible to take collective symbols and make use of them for political purposes as the Nazis did. To some extent, this is also what national advertising campaigns attempt to do—make use of collective symbols to sell a particular product. As we have noted, a living symbol gives expression to an unconscious element or factor. Thus, as Jung said, "The more widespread this factor is, the more general is the effect of the symbol, for it touches a corresponding chord in every psyche."[8]

Many of the collective symbols are religious images. The believer accepts them as revealed, as being of divine origin. The skeptic, however, insists that they have been invented. Jung said both were wrong—and also right. Religious symbols and concepts have been the object, for centuries, of careful and quite conscious elaboration, just as the skeptic discerns. But, on the other hand, it is also true that the origin of the symbolic aspect of such religious images is so deeply buried in the mystery of the past that they seem to have no human source. In such cases, Jung said, they were more like "collective representations, emanating from primeval dreams and creative fantasies. As such, these images are involuntary spontaneous manifestations and by no means intentional inventions."9

Basically, it could be said, a symbol is a bridge—bridging a gap between two things or two worlds. In the case of depth psychology, symbols are the bridge between the unconscious and the conscious. In mythology, symbols connect one reality with another— the everyday world of "now" and the world as it was in the beginning, in the "time of perfection." In religion, symbols connect the divine with the human, the infinite and ultimate with the finite and concrete. For all symbols there are these two aspects: there is the concrete, this world, conscious aspect, and there is the *other* to which it points and that it, in some way, also makes present.

So important was the role of symbols to Jung's thinking that he entitled the last book he was working on just before he died *Man and his Symbols*. In it, he said that it was the role of religious symbols to give meaning to our lives. To illustrate his point he referred to his experience in the American Southwest some years earlier. The Pueblo Indians, he said, believed that they were the children of Father Sun. This belief endowed their lives with a perspective that went far beyond their limited existence. Yet it left ample room for individual development. Jung said that their situation was far more satisfactory than that of a man in modern Western civilization who knows himself to be nothing more than an underdog, with no inner meaning to his life. "A sense of a wider meaning to one's existence," Jung wrote, "is what raises a man beyond mere getting and spending."[10] Without a sense of purpose and meaning one is "lost"—even as evangelical religion has always said about those outside the symbol system. Jung also cited St. Paul, who, he said, found his real and meaningful life in the inner certainty that he was the messenger of the Lord, and not merely a wandering weaver of carpets. As Jung said, "The myth that took possession of him made him something greater than a mere craftsman."[11] "Myth" for Jung (as we shall see in chapter 8) is a *living truth* (a psychic reality) that goes far beyond any materialstic reduction. Myth has the power that it does because it consists of *symbolic language*. It thereby connects two realities. That which is ultimate and infinite ("true always and everywhere") is made present in the limited and finite.

In distinguishing between individual and social symbols, Jung sometimes used the terms *natural* and *cultural* symbols. Natural symbols, he said, were derived from the unconscious contents of an individual psyche and could, therefore, represent an almost infinite number of variations on the essential archetypes of human experience. Cultural symbols are those that have been used to express "eternal truths" such as are found in the world's great religions. The latter have gone through many transformations, and even a long process of more or less conscious development.

The deterioration of symbols into mere signs is at least the by-product, if not the cause, of the situation in which we find ourselves today—often diagnosed as meaninglessness. In Jung's view, we have not realized how much our purely rational approach to everything has destroyed our capacity to respond to numinous symbols and ideas. While freeing ourselves from "superstition" by denying any validity to psychic reality, we thus put ourselves at the mercy of the psychic "underworld." The gods became diseases. We are now paying the price for the disintegration of our moral and spiritual tradition.

Jung pointed out that the anthropologists had called our attention to what happened in a primitive society when its spiritual values were exposed to the impact of modern civilization. We simply do not realize that we are now in the same condition: individuals find themselves without any meaning in their lives and social institutions are disintegrating. Jung placed the blame for our failure to understand what was happening on "our spiritual leaders," whom, Jung said, "unfortunately were more interested in protecting their institutions than in understanding the mystery that symbols present."[12] Faith and thought should not be antagonistic, Jung suggested. Unfortunately, too many believers were so afraid of science (and therefore psychology) that they turned a blind eye "to the numinous psychic powers that forever control man's fate. We have stripped all things of their mystery and numinosity: nothing is holy any longer."[13] With the disappearance of the holy, symbols become signs; there is no longer any opportunity for the uniting quality of symbols to be experienced.

Religion provides an especially striking and extremely widespread example of human symbolic activity. Religions throughout the world have made use of various phenomena of nature and human culture to serve as the symbolic devices through which complex meanings are conveyed. For example: particular sounds, made with the voice or with special instruments, ritual postures of all kinds, smells, colors, emblems and devices, and natural objects such as rivers, mountains, etc. As such, these phenomena not only "point" to something else, that is, "stand for it," but they actually make that other reality present for the worshipper—at least when they are still functioning as a symbol for the person and have not become a mere sign.

The problem, as Jung sees it, is that the personal experience of one individual (or a whole society) tends to fade in succeeding generations. It becomes a matter of "belief," to which one is expected to subscribe. William James, in his classic study *The Varieties of Religious Experience*, made a similar distinction when he spoke of those "individuals for whom religion exists not as a dull habit, but as an acute fever."[14]

When religious experience has become institutionalized, the uniting quality of the symbol tends to be present only in a secondary way. The symbol may still function as a "channelizer of psychic energy," but when encased in dogma (discussed in chapter 11) it tends to lose its power to grasp the individual throughout his or her being. As a mere intellectual concept, it is unable to resist the critic's reason. It becomes, as Freud taught, an *illusion*. While it is true that even Freud discerned the presence of something from the unconscious (he defined illusion as entailing desire, a wish fulfillment originating in the *id*), the unmistakable connotation of unreality remains. However, Freud correctly predicted the exodus which has occurred from those churches which have (what Freud called) "purified religious ideas"—that is, those churches which have left no room for an "otherness quality," or what William James called "piecemeal supernaturalism." With "purified religious ideas," all symbols become mere signs, and, as Freud said, "they will also lose their hold on human interest." [15] Jung, who, unlike Freud, valued religion as a psychotherapy, a healer of the soul, was critical of the general trend of Protestant liberal theology and its failure adequately to honor symbolic language. In a letter he wrote in 1951, Jung criticized the German New Testament theologian Rudolf Bultmann, whose program of demythologization he felt was a consequence of Protestant rationalism and led to an ever more progressive impoverishment of symbolism. If such a trend continued, he said, "Protestantism will become even more boring and penurious than it already is." [16]

It is the uniting quality of the symbol that led Jung to call it the "transcendent function." [17] It was the means by which unconscious contents could be related to consciousness. Thus, it was the means by which the ego could be in relation to that larger reality, which Jung called the *self*. For the Christian, symbolic language (the language of the sacraments) is the doorway to a living relationship with God. This aspect is discussed further in chapter 10.

Chapter Eight

MYTH AS MEANING-GIVER

It was Jung's conclusion that myths and fairy tales gave expression to unconscious processes. The retelling of the stories caused those processes to come alive again and be recollected, thus reestablishing the connection between the conscious and the unconscious.[1]

Jung's understanding of the function of myth is related to his concept of archetypes and the collective unconscious. Just as the human body has a common anatomy regardless of any racial differences, so too, Jung suggested, the human psyche possesses a common layer regardless of any differences in culture and consciousness. This "layer" (which Jung called the collective unconscious) explains why there are so many of the same symbols and mythological motifs to be found in varied parts of the world. It accounts for the universal in human experience: there is something about being human that has been true throughout human history and in all parts of the globe. There is a latent predisposition in all people toward an identical reaction to the same basic human situations. Jung thought that the various lines of psychic development started from one common stock whose roots reached far back into the distant past.[2]

Jung found it irritating at times that people seemed to assume that he had "dreamed up" the idea of archetypes and their presence in mythology. The universal occurrence of certain motifs in widely separated mythologies should be enough to suggest a theory of a common psychic heritage for mankind, Jung felt. But if not, he said, one had only to investigate the structure of schizophrenic delusions to discern that archetypal motifs occur in the psyches of people who have never heard of mythology.[3] In the BBC film *Face to Face*, Jung tells us that it was his own experience with a schizophrenic patient that pushed him in the direction of his theory of the collective unconscious. It was a hint, not proof, he said, but he "took the hint."

The motifs which Jung found being expressed in the dreams and other unconscious material of his patients were the same as those which one encountered in the world's fairy tales and in mythology. They were stories that expressed, and were about, *meaning*.

The human response has been, from the beginning, to describe the meaning of life in stories. In modern times our attention has been called to this function of story in human life by the anthropologists, although lovers of great literature had perhaps always unconsciously responded to this function. In *Magic, Science and Religion*, Malinowski wrote about the "special class of stories" to be found in primitive cultures.[4] These stories were regarded as sacred, and were embodied in the rituals, morals, and social organizations of a culture. The stories generally described a greater, usually primordial, and certainly a more relevant reality by which the present world was to be evaluated. The stories provided a reason for ritual and moral actions, and also described how to carry them out.

This type of story, one that functions in this way, is called *myth*. In the ordinary, everyday usage of the word, of course, *myth* means something that is "false" or "not real." It should be noted, however, that there are two ways in which the term *myth* is used: one is the popular usage, just mentioned, in which myth stands for the untrue; in the second way it is used it refers to a story that is infinitely true (in the way the anthropologists have described for us). In this latter usage, *myth* refers to a special kind of story that describes how life is and how life is to be responded to. This is the meaning of the term *myth* as used in this book.

We even speak of stories as being "true" whether they happened in a literal, historical sense or not. They are true if they describe what life is like. In fact, a really good story is one that could happen to anyone, anywhere, at any time. We may be glad it did not happen to us, or we may wish it had, but if it is a great story it describes what it means to *be*—how life is. And, in fact, whether we think it is a great story probably depends on whether we think life can be like that. It is other people's views about life (with which we disagree) that are "myths" (that is, in the everyday usage, false); *our* description of life is simply "true." Different cultures and different times in human history have had different points of view about what life is like, and they have had different cycles of stories to set these forth. Since all have been *human* experience, they often have the same or similar motifs. Jung revived the term *archetype* to refer to these great recurrent motifs of human experience, which have been expressed in different stories in different cultures and which he found also occur in the dreams of modern people.

Primitives did not *invent* myths, Jung said; they *experienced* them. Myths in fact were original revelations of the preconscious psyche. A tribe's basic set of stories constitutes its psychic life. A tribe disintegrates and falls to pieces when it loses its mythological heritage. As Jung said, "A tribe's mythology is its living religion, whose loss is always and everywhere, even among the civilized, a moral catastrophe."[5] Without myths, there is no link with the past and no basis for orientation toward the future. One is, indeed, "lost."

In *Myth and Reality*, Mircea Eliade, the historian of religions, called attention to the striking contrast between the way Western scholars today approach the study of myth and the way myth was regarded in the nineteenth century. Myth is no longer viewed as a "fable" or "invention," or even as "fiction," but, rather, it is accepted as it was in archaic societies, as not only a "true story," but, "beyond that, a story that is a most precious possession because it is sacred, exemplary, significant."[6]

Eliade says that in "archaic societies" myths supply models for human behavior. Repeatedly, anthropologists in the field were told, when asking about a particular behavior pattern, "We do it this way because the ancestor did it this way." Repetition is the keynote—in sharp contrast to the modern world, where it is the "new" that is aped! (Though one does come across, sometimes, the celebration of "The First Annual Whatever," which perhaps suggests that even today there is a feeling that it is *repetition* that lends importance and significance.) Eliade says that, in supplying models for human behavior, myths gave meaning and value to life for people in archaic societies.

Myth also provided a solution to the problem of *time* as the destroyer. For implicit in the perspective of the primitive was the notion of "the perfection of the beginning." Ancient Israel had its story of the Garden of Eden, and most peoples have had similar stories of a time of perfection in the beginning. People who lived then were "special," even giants or long-lived, certainly different in significant ways. A subsidiary notion is that *time destroys* that "perfection at the beginning." Ovid spoke of time as "the devourer" (*Metamorphoses*, XV, 234), and perhaps Shakespeare's most common image was that of devouring time.

If time is the problem, the destroyer, what is the solution? Memory. Memory is the way of healing, of overcoming time. Through myth and ritual, archaic societies recalled and reenacted the "original time," the time of the beginnings. Renewal rites are to be found in all religions. Traces of this way of thinking are still present in modern society, Eliade has suggested. Freud, for example, "discovered" memory as a method of healing the ravages of time. Psychoanalysis, in its classic Freudian form, involves remembering the events of childhood in order to be set free of unconscious forces. So also, in some Eastern religious disciplines, one of the last steps toward the goal of liberation from the wheel of rebirth involves remembering past lives.

Many religious ceremonies are "festivals of memory," telling us "who we are," among other things. They provide *identity*. "Forgetting" is the sacrilege! "If I forget you, O Jerusalem, let my right hand wither!" (Psalm 137:5) In Greek mythology the dead are those who have lost their memories. In Plato's theory of knowledge a "new" thought is a remembering from the eternal. Myths, as expressions of memory, gave meaning and value to life.

Joseph Campbell, editor of *The Portable Jung*, is perhaps even better known for his four-volume study of mythology, *The Masks of God*. In it, he identified four functions of mythology. He wrote, "The first and most distinctive—vitalizing all—is that of eliciting and supporting a sense of awe before the mystery of being."[7] Campbell cited Rudolf Otto's term *numinous* (used in *The Idea of the Holy*) as descriptive of this first function. On the primitive level, it is demonic dread; on the highest level, it is mystical rapture. This function of myth may be recognized, but it cannot be produced, Campbell says. Only the accident of experience or the symbolic language of a living myth can elicit and support it.

The *numinous* can, perhaps, be said to arise from a "sense of otherness." That which is strange and "other" is both fascinating and terrifying. In producing this sense of awe and wonder, myths provide access to power, emotional, psychological, and even physical reserves of power that are not otherwise available. (One does run faster when terrified!)

A second function of mythology is to provide an explanation or image of the universe and how it came to be, that is, a cosmology. The description of the world, however, has to correspond to the actual experience, knowledge, and mentality of the culture involved. This explanatory function of myth is what has given myth its "bad" name. Today we turn to science for explanations, rather than to the old folk stories of our culture. However, for most of us, science functions like myth in that we have no personal experience of the matter. We put our trust in the scientific view given us by our culture and enshrined in its myths. If asked why leaves are green, most of us would probably mutter something about "chlorophyll." But unless we were specialists, we would simply be repeating the *story* of someone else's experience. Similarly, with respect to Newton's laws, few of us know them to be true as a result of our own personal experience. We simply accept them as "facts" known to our culture. From time to time the "stories" have to be revised (and the textbooks rewritten)—for example, Newtonian physics has been modified.

A third function of mythology is a sociological one. Myths help to relate an individual to the group. They make individuals feel that they belong. They know "who they are"—"sons of the covenant," "children of the sun goddess Ame-te-ra-su," and so on. The opening song in *Fiddler on the Roof* makes the point under discussion: "Tradition, where everyone knows who he is, and what God expects him to do!" It is in the stories of their cultures that individuals in primitive societies found their orientation and direction—how they were to live. These provided them with a justification for their *values.* "This is the thing to do because it was done this way by the ancestors." But, since primitive times, there has been a gradual enlarging of the group, and this has meant that numerous national, racial, class, and even religious mythologies have become "out of date"—no longer relevant in the enlarged world. The people of ancient Israel in exile asked themselves, "How can we sing the Lord's song in a strange land?" Could their God, Yahweh, be worshipped hundreds of miles away from the Promised Land and with His Temple destroyed? The world's so-called "great religions" are those that were able to transcend the concrete, localized expression of the truth about life they had discerned. One way of viewing the problems of world peace today is to note that in the new reality of one world shared by all people around the globe there is no common set of stories that provides a common identity. Space travel may help to give us a sense of "we earthmen," but in the meantime we have a problem with the absence of this unifying function of myth. (The popularity of the television series *Star Trek* and the motion picture *Star Wars* may have something to say to this point.)

Another aspect of this sociological function of myth can be seen in the help myth and ritual provide by indicating how to meet crises of various kinds. Routines are helpful! If we can do habitual things at times of crises, it is a help. Social customs (such as those that prevail at funerals) help us to bear the grief or terrors or whatever else that come upon us. Also, they provide ways of indicating to others that we are "with them" in their problem, regardless of any religious orientation.

A fourth function of mythology is to help the individual learn something about him- or herself. This is the psychological function of mythology. Myths traditionally have something to say about the proper course for one's inner development. Perhaps it is this function (even more than the third) which contemporary society finds missing. The question continues to plague us: "Who am I?" The problem of self-identity is basic, nearly all social scientists tell us. Despite a strong emphasis on individualism, we have a problem with our personal significance. What is the meaning of *my* life? How can we find a purpose and meaning that will hold up in all the circumstances that arise in life? Most of the variety of things we choose to give ourselves seem to fail us in the end. Our awareness of the relativity of all cultural goals leaves us with a problem of emptiness and meaninglessness. We feel the absence of a "larger reality" to which we are, or can be, related. Those of course for whom a religious tradition is still a *living reality* do not have this particular dis-ease.

The functions of mythology that we have been reviewing are, of course, the functions that religion has traditionally performed. Thus, myth (in this special sense we have been examining) can be said to be part of the *language* of religion. Religions provide a picture of a "larger reality." There is "something more" beyond one's own limited personal experience. In all places and in all times, people have found values that gave significance to their lives and lifted them out of the humdrum of daily existence. And the only way this kind of transcendent value can be talked about is in stories—the language of myth and symbol.

The South African author Laurens Van der Post, in writing about the Bushmen, whom he calls "the first men of Africa," said, "These people knew what we do not: that without a story you have not got a nation, or a culture, or a civilization."[8] The Bushmen's stories were the supreme expression of their spirit, and so, their most sacred possession.

There are some truths about life that can only be described in story, and it is for stories with this kind of understanding that the term *myth* is especially useful. For example, how can you talk about a reality that most people have considered very important—love? Can you do it without telling a story of some sort? You certainly cannot say, concretely, that it is green and weighs three pounds! Do you not finally have to tell a story—perhaps about an individual who lays down his life for another?

Love, justice, courage, truth, mercy, compassion—these are the kind of values that transcend any concrete, material expression of them. They demand to be illustrated. Whatever values have grasped a people as the basic theme of and truths about life and about a response to life have been set forth in a series of stories. The answer or answers that they discern can only be grasped in story form. Certainly this was true in the beginning. Stories were the means by which primitive peoples discerned the realities of life and learned the means of coping with those realities.

The Jungian analyst Frances Wickes, in the introduction to her book *The Inner World of Choice*, wrote: "Modern man is unaware of the myth that lives itself within him, of the image, often invisible, that dynamically impels him toward choice."[9] Yet, she goes on to say, he lives out a myth in the way he meets the inner and outer events of his life. In fact, to know another's myth is to know his innermost desires, goals, and the basis for his choices.

Many students in our world today think "fiction" is not worthy of serious attention. What does it have to do with "real life" (that is, with "making a living")? However, it is beginning to occur to many (who have tried to live in a demythologized world) that the kind of truth about which we have been speaking is best expressed in story form. Perhaps that is why a demythologized world has been found to be a meaningless world. Humanity without myth is indeed, as the title of one of Jung's collection of essays suggests, "modern man in search of a soul." The kind of story which provides "soul," which mediates a meaning and value to life, is what Jung meant by *myth*.

Living a story, whether it be "the old, old story" of Christian hymnody that grasps us, or some new image of truth that reveals itself to us, is the way we experience meaning and value in our lives. Living a story (finding, as Jung says, "our myth") is what provides us with the framework for choosing the values we will serve.

Chapter Nine

RELIGIOUS EXPERIENCE
AS A UNION OF OPPOSITES

C. G. Jung taught that the psychic experiences that give joy and meaning in life, that indeed make life possible in any meaningful sense, involve a *union of opposites*, a reconciliation of opposing possibilities. If Jung is right, his observation constitutes a major contribution to the psychology of religion. Furthermore, it should have a profound effect upon theologizing, not to mention the Church's understanding of its evangelical task. What I have sought to do in this chapter is: first, to explicate Jung's insight, and secondly, to try to understand how, from what we know about religious experience in general, his insight about the union of opposites can be seen as correct, or at least as heuristically useful.

Psychology of religion textbooks have floundered over the question of a definition of religion ever since the time of William James, who in his famous *The Varieties of Religious Experience* (1902) suggested that the very fact that we had so many different definitions should be enough to tell us that the word "religion" could not stand for any single principle or essence, but rather was a collective name.[1] James concluded that religion, broadly speaking, "consists of the belief that there is an unseen order, and that our supreme good lies in harmoniously adjusting ourselves thereto."[2] Religion then, following James, could be said to be simply the response we make to the realities of life as we perceive them.

Certainly religion is more than what goes on in churches, synagogues, and temples, although it often is an institutional arm of the establishment. From earliest times, the medicine man and the tribal chief, if indeed not the same person, have at least been in alliance in support of their culture. Constantine, the first Christian emperor of the Roman empire, was not the first nor the last to feel that unity in religious belief among his armies was a helpful factor—and worth the expense of calling the first Christian Council at Nicea in A.D. 325. Intolerance of "dissenters" from the religious establishment of Reformation England led many a person to the American colonies. It was this aspect of religion as an arm of the establishment that led Karl Marx to call religion "the opiate of the people." However, from the prophets of ancient Israel to the Berrigan brothers of the Vietnam War, religion has also been the instrument or arm of social protest. For Moses and Martin Luther King Jr., it was the rallying cry for liberation from social oppression.

Religion is also more than some special kind of belief. In the beginning of comparative religious studies this was the most common premise from which these studies proceeded. For some people, if asked, religion has to do with a particular kind of belief, such as life after death or belief in a supreme being. For others, religion is the acceptance of a moral order and living by it. This emphasis on morality, however, is largely a Western bias—a Western presupposition about what religions are all about. Again, this kind of approach focuses on the social order and the necessity for some rules if people are to be able to live with each other. Despite sociological studies about the role of religion, it is more than the "glue" that holds a society together.

Rudolf Otto gave a new direction in religious studies with his book *The Idea of the Holy* (1923), which focused on the *irrational* as the factor all religions had in common. Otto called this irrational factor the *numinosum*. By this he referred to a dynamic agency or effect not caused by an arbitrary act of will. Both fascination and awe are qualities associated with the numinous. "Reverence," for example, as a religious attitude, includes, at least in part, an act of will. Otto sought to identify an involuntary experience.

In the spirit of the broad kind of approach taken by William James and Rudolf Otto, Paul Tillich spoke of religion as a "being grasped by an ultimate concern."[3] Tillich's definition has the merit of recognizing that religion is something more than merely a rational enterprise. To regard religion as a matter of intellectual ideas is, in Tillich's vocabulary, "the intellectualistic distortion of faith."[4] "Being grasped" suggests the role of the unconscious, of feelings.

In his Terry lectures at Yale in 1937, Jung said, "Religion, as the Latin word denotes, is a careful scrupulous observation of what Rudolf Otto aptly termed the *numinosum*."[5] Religious experience, for Jung, is something that happens to the person. The human subject is more the victim than the creator of such an experience. Thus, for Jung, religion is always a *personal* experience of the psyche.

While the ego is the center of consciousness, as Jung defined it, it is not the center of the psyche. "As I see it," Jung said, "the psyche is a world in which the ego is contained."[6] The ego encounters *interference* with its plans, its intentions. St. Paul described one aspect of this in the seventh chapter of his letter to the Romans—how he found himself doing what he did not intend to do and vice versa. A more positive encounter is the Christian experience of God's Holy Spirit "coming down" and possessing the human spirit.[7] All religions have some means of conceptualizing the ego's encounter with an "other," whether understood in theistic terms or not.

From a psychological point of view, Jung said, we must understand these experiences of an "other" as being in, through, or from the unconscious. The unconscious is simply that which is not in consciousness. It is the unknown. "No man has seen God," scripture says. In the biblical tradition, it is understood that we only know God as God reveals himself to us. Revelation is, in Jung's view, an experience of, or "from," the unconscious. The essence of religion, from a psychological point of view, Jung said, is to give practical consideration to those processes by which the ego is affected.

When Jung spoke about the apprehension of God in the psyche, he was not talking about an *idea*. Jung was ready to agree with Freud that, at least for some people, their *idea* of God was nothing more than a projection of childhood dependency needs. But Jung moved beyond a *psychopathology* of religion. God is something that is *experienced*, if one but knows it—if one "has ears to hear," as Jesus might have said. God is something that has an effect on one, not something of one's own creation. In his writing, Jung usually spoke of the "God-image" in the psyche, rather than simply "God," as he wanted to make clear that he was always at least attempting to limit what he said to what the psyche experiences, that is, to what we can *know*. It should be obvious, Jung said, that when he spoke of an "imprint" on the psyche that something caused it, but about the nature of the "imprinter" psychology had nothing to say.[8] One needs to keep in mind that Jung did *not* say that the individual creates God. Rather, he suggested that it is a suprapersonal function of the psyche that creates the God-image.

When the whole history of mankind is taken into consideration, the "interferences" from the unconscious that the ego has encountered can be seen to fall into certain patterns or motifs. Jung called such patterns *archetypes*. He was not speaking about "inherited ideas" in the psyche, but rather of "dramas" that were shaped and imaged by the particular culture and personal life history of the individual.

The central archetype of the psyche is what Jung called the *self*. It is the psychic totality of an individual. He said, "Anything that a man postulated as being a greater totality than himself can become a symbol of the self."[9] Thus, in theistic religions, in Jung's thought, any incarnation or self-manifestation of God functions for a person in that religion as a symbol of the self. In Christianity, the Christ is a symbol of the self; in Judaism, the expected Messiah or Messianic Age has functioned at times, and for some, as a symbol of the self. In Buddhism, the Buddha or the Buddha nature functions as a symbol of the self.

The archetype of the self is encountered in symbols of totality and wholeness. It is the *God-image* experienced by the ego, and Jung used the two expressions interchangeably. As a symbol, the self necessarily includes a union of opposites: male and female, dark and light, good and evil. To call the self a *God-image* points to the way the self is encountered by the ego—that is, as all-powerful, all-knowing, authoritative, and so on. But to call the self a *God-image* is also to suggest, at least implicitly and to all but the most meticulous reader, that the God of the theologians, the metaphysical God, has those same attributes. And indeed, Jung also argued in his later writing, if Christianity was monotheistic (and not dualistic), that must be so as well. This question is explored further in chapters 14 and 15.

Jung came to understand neurosis as an inner cleavage, rather like being at war with oneself. Anything that accentuated the cleavage made the patient worse, and anything that mitigated it tended to heal. The problem lay in the person's experience of two forces in opposition to each other. Jung said, "The conflict may be between the sensual and the spiritual man, or between the ego and the shadow." [10] St. Paul described his own experience of a split within himself in a similar way: "I do not understand my own actions. For I do not do what I want, but I do the very thing I hate." (Romans 7:15) For St. Paul, the solution was a religious experience. And Jung, too, called the healing of such a split a religious problem. Jung said that if we were ready to recommend the Christian virtue of forgiveness and love of one's enemies in the sphere of social or national problems, we should be ready to do the same inwardly, in the treatment of neurosis. The modern individual wants to hear no more about guilt and sin, Jung said. Rather, he is concerned with his own pressing problem—namely, how "to reconcile himself with his own nature—how he is to love the enemy in his own heart and call the wolf his brother."[11]

Religious experience involves a healing of that split which is so characteristic of the general neurosis of people today. Jung's message was that we must accept ourselves. We must find a way to live our own lives and remain true to ourselves, to our own inner calling, just as Jesus lived his own life and remained true to himself. For Jung, this was the true meaning of the "imitation of Christ."

If one follows a path of accepting oneself and of listening to the unconscious (the latter being a necessary step if one is to know just who it is one is accepting in accepting oneself) and thus coming to terms with "the other side," then, Jung found, guidance seems to come from the unconscious by means of a reconciling symbol in and through which the opposites are overcome and the split is healed. The new synthesis is like a third position. The previous sense of confusion is dissipated. The person finds, Jung said in describing the experience, that "he can accept the conflict within him and so come to resolve the morbid split in his nature on a higher level."[12] St. Paul was perhaps describing a similar experience when he said, "the fruit of the Spirit is love, joy, peace, patience, kindness, goodness, faithfulness, gentleness, self-control." (Galatians 5:22–23)

Jung's diagnosis of the psyche, was, as we have seen, that it is characterized by a tension of opposites, and that, indeed, this is the source of psychic energy. That this must be so follows from the nature of consciousness, which is a discrimination between this and that. He also discerned a "push" toward wholeness, or completion. This development he called, as we have noted, the path of individuation. This movement toward wholeness, toward overcoming the split, was perhaps discerned by Freud, as he spoke in his later writings of a "death instinct" in the psyche. If the tension of opposites is the source of psychic energy, a complete overcoming of the split would, of course, mean the cessation of psychic energy, or "Death."

Jung, however, understood this tension of opposites as a basic attribute of life, and further, that life does push toward a resolution, toward an experience of wholeness. It is true that the overcoming of the split is a kind of death and rebirth experience. A *sacrifice* is involved, as man's folk wisdom has always known. The ego has a "death experience" in its encounter with the self. But it also opens up the possibilities of new life.

An encounter with the self is an experience of the overcoming of the split; it is a union of opposites, as Jung understood it. A third position is achieved. It is a synthesis, where formerly there was thesis and antithesis. The synthesis is achieved by a uniting symbol. That is why Jung spoke of the symbol as the transcendent function.

Salvation means healing. The world's great systems for healing the psyche have been the world's great religions, as Jung said. They are systems of salvation. Religous experience ultimately for Jung was an experience of the union of opposites. That is what gives it the *numinous* quality, the sense of "otherness." Let me try to illustrate how I understand some of the world's great religious symbol systems to have functioned in helping the individual accept him or herself—a basic task in Jung's analysis.

What is "new" in the New Testament? What is the distinctive teaching of Jesus? All of Jesus' teachings can be found in one form or another in the sayings of the great rabbis preserved in the Talmud. One of my former colleagues, Professor Ben Zion Netanyahu, when posing this question, suggested that what was "new" in Jesus' teachings was the extreme position he took with respect to forgiveness. "Love your enemies," he said, was not a teaching to be found in the rabbinical writings. Christian theologians have called this the experience of "unconditional acceptance" by God. "While we were yet sinners Christ died for us," St. Paul says, in wonder. The peculiar Christian experience—the "good news"—which the early Christian community proclaimed to all who would listen was that God loves us—even though I know and he knows what I am like! In this experience, there is a coming together of opposites—the awareness of unacceptableness and an experience of acceptance. This, it seems to me, is the basic message of the Christian story; it is the fundamental "good news" that every heart longs to hear. The message is presented in a *story*, of course, as all such ultimate truths must be, as was discussed in chapter 8. One perhaps has to conceptualize existence with the images and categories that the story makes use of before the message of the story can grasp us. For finally, as Jung said, it is not a matter of our "belief," but of our experience. It happens; we are "grasped" by the truth.

In the history of American Protestantism, *salvation preaching* involved making the "sinner" aware that he or she was a sinner—separated from God. The idea is indicated by the title of one of the famous sermons of the early American preacher Jonathan Edwards—"Sinners in the Hands of an Angry God." Part of the process in such preaching involves making the hearer aware of the opposites. The first step is to be reminded that we are sinful, that our pride and selfishness have led us farther and farther away from our calling. The second step involves hearing again the story of God's goodness, which is so extreme. (As the story reminds us, God sent his only son to us and he died for us. What greater love is there than when one lays down his life for another?) The third step is the proclamation of the great good news that a reconciliation of the two is not only possible, but indeed has already been accomplished!

In the Cross, the reconciling symbol (which even involves a coming together of two lines moving in opposite directions), we have a symbol that (through the story in which it participates) holds together the two opposites: sinful humanity who has denied God, and the loving God who forgives them and takes them back.

That is the Christian story (the Christian "myth" as we have come to call it in chapter 8). The classic Christian experience is surely that of a union of opposites.

I cannot speak from firsthand experience here, but in so far as I can discern the basic religious experience of Judaism, it seems to be something like this. Again, the basic point is quite similar, as one would expect in two sister religions. It is a matter of God's *acceptance*. But here the story, the myth of meaning, centers on God's choice of a particular people. The people are aware that they are quite insignificant compared to the great political powers around them, but the choice fell on *them*. In the mist of prehistory, there are the patriarchs. Abraham was chosen and given a land. Next the choice fell on Isaac and not Ishmael, then Jacob and not Esau—despite Jacob's treachery! It was not a matter of being "good" or "worthy"! Through Moses they were "delivered," despite a lot of bickering and unfaithfulness on the journey out. David, the great king, was chosen by God—"a man after God's own heart"—yet David had Bathsheba's husband sent to the front lines, where he might be killed, in order to add Bathsheba to his harem. Then there are the prophets of ancient Israel, who do not hesitate to point out, in the most trenchant terms, Israel's sinfulness, yet also proclaiming, equally fervently, God's love of his people.

In this story too, we have the coming together of opposites—the awareness of unacceptableness and the experience of acceptance. Knowing that by divine choice and intention one has been singled out from the beginning of the world is enough to give one a feeling of dignity and importance and to lift one beyond the transitoriness and meaninglessness of ordinary human existence, Jung said.[13] Judaism has a role to play, according to its religious story, in the divine world drama. To be a part of this people is to be in covenant relationship with God, and thereby, through that identity, to experience the power and strength of being acceptable, in an ultimate sense.

Jung found the most intriguing illustration of religious experience as the union of opposites expressed in the rich symbolism of alchemy, which he spent the latter years of his life exploring. Alchemy, he said, could be compared to a religious rite. The difference lay in the fact that alchemy, unlike the creedal statements of a church, was not a rigorously defined collective activity, but rather, an individual work requiring the utmost commitment. It was a work of reconciliation between apparently incompatible opposites. Furthermore, alchemists understood the opposition as being not merely the natural hostility of the physical elements with which they worked, but involving a moral conflict as well. The alchemist still lived in a world that included psychic reality as well as physical reality. The split between spirit and matter, about which Jung has written at length, had not proceeded so far as to render the alchemist unaware of both aspects of nature. On the contrary, alchemical work was to achieve that unity and integration which the alchemist understood to be the direction and purpose of nature. Writing about alchemy in an epilogue to one of his last books, *Mysterium Coniunctionis*, Jung said, "Its goal consisted in a symbol which had an empirical and at the same time a transcendental aspect."[14] In alchemy, Jung thought, we had an example of how individuals of another age sought to make the "connection," to relate through their symbols the unconscious with consciousness, to relate God to the individual. For most people today the split is so deep they have come to ignore one side—psychic reality. Only the physical is accepted as "real."

The whole task of the individuation process involves a reintegration of the opposites—of integrating aspects of the unconscious into consciousness. Symbolically, it might be said that, in ultimate terms, the union of opposites (as the task of life) moves toward a bringing into relationship of those "ultimate opposites," God and the individual person. That is why Jung said the alchemists themselves viewed their work as a *religious* work.

With the religious symbol systems of the East, the categories are often largely nontheistic and nonpersonal. It is not a matter of overcoming a "separation" (between God and the individual person), but rather of the contrast between the One and the Many, of how to be "at one" (is it still "atonement"?) in the midst of the "ten-thousand-and-one" things of everyday existence. It is still, perhaps one can see, a problem of the union of opposites, as Jung maintained.

Jung viewed our long evolutionary history as a story of evolving consciousness. In the West, Christianity had a key place in the story. In his essay "Transformation Symbolism in the Mass," Jung described how the Mass might well be called the rite of the individuation process. The Mass, he said, was the end product of a long development that, "with the progressive broadening and deepening of consciousness, gradually made the isolated experience of specifically gifted individuals the common property of a larger group." [15] What had earlier been the prerogative of the Pharaohs only, and later, in the mystery religions of Greece, something not to be talked about, gradually broadened out into a collective experience. The underlying psychic process was not described as such, but was dramatized in the form of "mysteries" and "sacraments," which were reinforced by suitable religious teachings, meditations, and acts of sacrifice. The whole process worked to make the initiate feel intimately connected with the mythic happenings. The broadening of consciousness, the withdrawal of some projections, the awareness of the shadow, the strengthening of the ego, and the consequent assumption of responsibility for choices made moved away from being simply the experience of the upper classes, or those who could afford the expense and time of a journey to a place of initiation. Christianity sought to introduce as many people as possible to the experience of the mystery. So, as soon as possible, the celebration of the mysteries was made a public institution. (Christianity was illegal in the Roman empire until Constantine's Edict of A.D. 312.) With this development, Jung said, the individual eventually "could not fail to become conscious of his own transformation and of the necessary psychological conditions for this, such as confession and repentance of sin." [16]

The experience of the self is an experience of the union of opposites in Jung's thought, and it is, in fact, what is meant by "religious experience." Jung included, of course, personal, individual experiences of a uniting symbol as encountered in dreams. While the world's great religions used a different language, Jung said, they spoke of the same experience that he and many other psychologists had encountered. "All confirm," he wrote, "the existence of a compensatory ordering factor which is independent of the ego and whose nature transcends consciousness." [17]

This ordering factor, which, as Jung said, is independent of the ego, itself encompasses a union of opposites, and the *encounter* with the self in the individual human psyche is experienced as a reconciliation of opposing possibilities within the person (a union of opposites)—whether it be the awareness of an acceptance of unacceptableness, or the awareness of a unity and cosmic harmony despite the disharmony of human existence.

PART III

Jung's Challenge to Christianity

Chapter Ten

THE LANGUAGE OF RELIGION

Jung challenged Christianity in regard to a number of issues, but the underlying themes of these challenges could be said to be: (a) for Christians to recognize the fact that symbolical language is the necessary language of religion, and (b) for Christians to appreciate their treasurehouse of religious symbolism and to set about recovering its meaning for people today. There is some indication that institutional Christianity is responding to this need—although not without protests from those who find change too painful. Throughout the various branches of Christendom in recent years interest has focused on updating the language of the Church. This was a major aspect of Pope John's *aggiornamento*, of the Episcopalians' revision of the Book of Common Prayer, and of the numerous conferences on liturgy and the language of worship throughout Protestantism. One aspect of this concern, which has come to the fore in recent years, is the presence of sexist language in worship.

The language of religion must be that language that relates the human to the infinite, to the ultimate, to God. The problem of meaning—so pervasive for us today—is ultimately solved in the feeling of relatedness to something "larger" than oneself. The world built by the ego's own striving and willing is not enough. We long for something more. Jung wrote, "The decisive question for man is: Is he related to something infinite or not? That is the telling question of his life." [1] We need to know that what is important to us truly matters—that is, has infinite significance. That is the only way we can avoid setting our minds on futilities and all kinds of goals of no real importance. Thus, we may demand that the world grant us recognition for our talent or beauty—qualities that we regard as our personal possessions. But, Jung said, the less sensitive we are to what is essential, the less satisfying are our lives. We feel limited because we have limited aims. Envy and jealousy soon become our companions. On the other hand, if we can feel that our lives are linked with the infinite, our desires and attitudes change. It is the task of any religious tradition to help the individual make the connection. Christianity can do this only by using the language of religion.

In his teaching, Jesus used vivid imagery drawn from the everyday life experience of his listeners. The medieval Church, responding to a largely illiterate people, used a world of vaulting cathedrals, stained glass windows, statues, and art of all kinds to communicate the Christian message. The stories of past great Christians, the saints, helped to communicate the kind of response called for in a variety of situations. But with the arrival of the printing press, followed shortly by the Protestant Reformation and the great schism in the Western Church, the focus of concern moved more toward concepts and definitions—toward setting the boundaries and limits of belief. The Reform and Lutheran traditions in northern Europe were concerned with drawing up "Confessions," which were statements of belief or creeds. The Counter-Reformation of Catholic Europe also, for decades at the Council of Trent, engaged in drawing up definitions and articles of faith. The whole movement away from a recognition of the necessarily symbolic language of Christianity reached a culmination in the nineteenth century with the adoption in biblical study of the presuppositions of the physical sciences—namely, a mechanistic world view. Yet, even as theologians and biblical scholars were abandoning the traditional holistic approach of the humanities (so essential in art and literature) for the literalistic, piecemeal analytic approach (appropriate in the physical sciences), depth psychology was calling attention to the fact of psychic reality and the necessity of symbolic language for the understanding of human experience.

"Concepts are coined and negotiable values; images are life," Jung wrote.[2] Myth, symbol, and ritual have always been the language of religion, Jung said, and if Christianity would speak to us today it must realize this truth. From Jung's point of view, the theological program of Rudolf Bultmann, *demythologization,* was not only a hopeless task, but misconceived. Myth consists of events that are continually repeated and can be observed over and over again. Myth, as Jung said, is something that *happens* to us.[3] We long for the experience of *connection,* of feeling related to something larger than ourselves. Only that language that will give expression to that experience will suffice. If Christianity abandons the language of religion, it no longer speaks to the human heart. Dag Hammarskjöld expressed a similar understanding when he wrote, "The language of religion is a set of formulas which register a basic spiritual experience."[4] The reality of that experience is accessible to our senses, but we should not attempt to analyze the language used to describe the experience with terms defined by philosophy and the tools of logic, he said.

Religion is, as was suggested in chapter 9, basically our response to life. It is what we live by and for. All of us have concerns, things upon which we make decisions. Sometimes we have to choose. Some concerns are more important to us than others, and then the choice is easy. If we have lived long enough and found some order or centering in our lives, we will have developed a kind of pyramid or hierarchy of concerns. Whatever is at the top of our priority list of concerns is functioning as a "god" in a sense—it may be the God of biblical religions or it may be our "belly," as St. Paul suggested was the case for some people. For many of us something is ultimate, that is, lies beyond all other concerns. As Jung wrote, "One could even define religious experience as that kind of experience which is accorded the highest value, no matter what its contents may be."[5]

The danger is that we may take as our chief value in life something that is finite, such as another person, or physical pleasures, or a business enterprise. Such a "god" may fail us or evade us, and then we are in trouble. We are indeed "lost" in every sense. The top value on our priority list of concerns needs to be something that lasts, that is over and beyond the everyday. Love, truth, justice—these are values that partake of the infinite, that are beyond the finite limitations of human life. They are also the values that have found expression in most of the great religions—in polytheistic religions sometimes as gods or goddesses themselves, and in the biblical religions, as attributes of the one God.

How can the infinite, that which is "beyond," be expressed? The answer is: only with symbolical language. Symbols have this character, as we have seen, of bridging two worlds.

Through symbolic language, the infinite or ultimate may be expressed, and indeed, be made present for us in a finite or concrete image. It can, of course, never be taken "only concretely." Few Christians would understand the reference in the Nicene Creed to Christ's "sitting on the right hand of the Father" as something to be taken literally. No one argues about the nature of the chair or bench. Yet, "sitting on the right hand of the Father" expresses profoundly the truth of our experience that the Christ is ultimately important. To take this expression in the creed "only concretely" would be to affirm one's confidence about the seating arrangement in the heavenly throne room, but it would say nothing about the meaning of Christ in our lives.

There is a tendency to say "only a symbol," and Christians have, at times, felt that something *less* than their experience was being expressed when the language used was called "symbolical."[6] Yet the opposite is the case. *Less* is expressed if we see the image "only concretely."

The tendency to say "only a symbol" is a product of our materialistic approach to all of reality. This tendency fails to recognize what Jung called "psychic reality." In our century, with the rise of psychotherapy, we have begun to recognize that psychic pain, such as grief or the necessity for a "hard choice," can be just as incapacitating as the loss of a leg or a broken wrist. However, we are, as a people in the West, still reluctant to carry over the recognition of psychic reality into the area of values and meaning—the area of religion. This reluctance arises in part from the fact that the biblical religions witness historically to specific (concrete) expressions of ultimate truth at given times and places. This should not, however, preclude those events from being appreciated symbolically. In other words, it is possible for the truth of myth to be expressed in history.

If our relationship with God must be expressed symbolically, because symbolic language alone is able to express that which is infinite or ultimate, then how are the concrete expressions of that relationship to be regarded? The god may be present for his people in the sacred tree or the sacred temple building, but if the tree or the building is destroyed, has the god been destroyed? People experience the presence of the divine; once experienced, this reality cannot be questioned. The infinite or ultimate may be "present" in the concrete object, but the concrete object cannot be equated with the ultimate. To do so is *idolatry*—treating something less than God as God.

The leaders of ancient Israel had to face this problem after the Babylonian Exile. Was their God, Yahweh, "bigger" than his Temple, which had been destroyed? Could the Lord be worshipped in a strange land? Success in surviving the materialistic distortion is perhaps what enables a religion to become a "great religion" that speaks to many people over a long period of history.

A symbol has a double aspect or uniting quality. It is a concretely present thing that points to something beyond itself, and yet it also participates in some way in that to which it points. When something does not have, or has lost, for us, that "participative" quality, then it is not a symbol for us. That is what has happened to the sacraments for many Catholics, as well as Protestants.

Myth and symbol, then, are of necessity the language of religion. Many Christians have trouble with the word *myth* because of its customary usage. They do not object to Jesus' teaching in parables—a special kind of story—but to name as *myth* the kind of story by which religious truth is expressed all over the world seems to them to detract from the uniqueness of its *saving quality*, which they personally have experienced and therefore *know* to be true. Jung, like the historians of religion, recognized that while any religious truth is uniquely true (and an historical experience!) for the person for whom it expresses a saving expression, still, if one is to be able to discuss religious experience in general, one needs a term to describe the particular kind of story that has this power.

Modern Christians face a dilemma: How can we both have myths (as we must to be religious) and at the same time know that they are myths (as we must if we are modern)?[7] The thoughtful Christian knows that the relationship with God (whom we know to be "beyond," infinite, ultimate, etc.) can only be expressed in symbolic or mythical language. Yet many are afraid that to call the expression of that relationship a "story," and even a "myth" is to suggest that it is not true in some way. We have to look more closely.

Some stories are true (life is like that), and some stories are not true (life is not like that). The "truth" of the story in the religious sense is not dependent upon whether it has been enacted in history ("really" happened, as we are likely to say). The religious truth certainly is not dependent upon the particular details or "window dressing" of the story—although these are essential if it is to remain an effective story. (Recall the two aspects of any symbol.)

Stories are essential to describe the Christian experience and, indeed, were used by Jesus to describe what our relationship to God could be like. Further, the committed Christian "knows" (whatever imagery is used to describe the reality of the experience) that he or she has an inner connection or relationship with the divine that has changed his or her whole perspective on life. Most likely these Christians not only use the imagery with which they are familiar to describe the reality, but that is, in fact, the way their psyches actually experience the connection or relationship. For example, it may be the experience of being born again (John 3:7), receiving the Holy Spirit (Acts 2:4), experiencing reconciliation with God (II Corinthians 5:19), experiencing an "inner light" (George Fox and the Quaker tradition), having one's heart "strangely warmed" (John Wesley), or having a vision of the Lady of all mercy and the One to whom God will listen (Marian devotion in centuries of Catholic tradition). To take any of the imagery used to portray the Christian experience "only concretely" is to destroy the main point. It describes a felt reality. As such, it is "true," and is a part of our history.

The early Christians experienced the reality of a new relationship with God, which they described in various ways. Their experience centered around Jesus, whom they knew either "in the flesh" (as Paul said) or from their encounter with the risen Christ or his Holy Spirit. In him, God had acted. Some years later, their descriptions were collected, along with the remembered sayings of Jesus, and the beginnings of the New Testament came into being. It *was* a new testament, a new covenant, a new basis of relationship with God. There were stories describing how this relationship could come into being, how it had been experienced, and, using the imagery of the day, how it could be understood.

Christians have had trouble (mostly with each other) when they stopped focusing on the basic reality and sought to set limits to it, that is, to compose definitions. (To *define* means, literally, to fix boundaries or limits to.) To choose one description of God's saving presence in the life of an individual and to emphasize that alone (or as opposed to some other description of God's healing presence) is to create unnecessary divisions. It is like missing the forest by focusing only on a tree.

The New Testament is a mixture of all kinds of stories and imagery. The main focus is on what God has done: a new testament or covenant, that is, a new basis for relationship has been provided. That is the "good news" being proclaimed. Understood symbolically (whether historically or not), all of the stories and images proclaim this central truth. It was a great victory for what C. S. Lewis might call the Church's "enemy" when Christians were persuaded to apply the test of "history" to the source of their knowledge of the "good news." This is not to say that the basic facts were not historical, but they were intertwined in language that was concerned with proclamation rather than history as we have come to think of it. It is futile to attempt to reconcile obvious contradictions in some of the stories in the Bible. Yet, they are not contradictions if we see them for what they are—attempts to portray the experiences of a people in their relationship with God.

For Jung and others in our day, to call a story a myth is to pay it a compliment. It is to recognize the story as one dealing with matters of ultimate, indeed divine, significance.

To function as a myth, a story has to express our encounter with reality. The basic Christian myth is a story of how God created our world and found his creation to be good. In the course of time, and almost from the beginning, the world, in its freedom, became separated, alienated from its Creator. Yet God so loved the world that at a particular time, now long ago, he sent his Son, not to condemn, but to redeem the world through the power of love. In our state of separation (sin), we killed the very One he sent. God's love, however, was not thwarted. The story goes on to say that God demonstrated the power of love by using that death as a means of our salvation, raising the One he sent from the grave, empowering us with his own Holy Spirit, and offering us also a new life as participants in his new creation, the Church, the body of Christ's resurrection.

The thoughtful Christian will recognize the imaginative character of the story's language. To speak of God as "sending" his son, or of the "exchange" of his life for our sin, is to use images which cannot be taken "only concretely." It is a story. Yet it is a true story for the Christian, who knows, from his or her own experience, that what the story describes actually occurred, and still occurs, for in that new community, the new covenant, he or she has experienced reconciliation and inner healing—a new life.

In our day the power of *story* is beginning to be recovered. There is a new emphasis on how stories put us in touch with meaning—indeed, give meaning to our lives. Jung was one of the first to write, in his autobiography, about finding his own myth of meaning, his own story. Fantasy literature has helped us to break out of the "only concrete." Hollywood has discovered a rich box office in stories about ultimate meaning, about the continual struggle between good and evil—even on a cosmic level.

Relearning how to find meaning for our day in our priceless heritage of stories is what Christianity should be doing. In the days before nearly universal literacy, Christians were well acquainted with the use of imagery and symbolical language. The problem arose when, in the West, we began to take things "only concretely," when people began to say "that didn't *really* happen." Children's libraries became greatly impoverished. A diet of pure materialistic "facts" is a starvation diet. Thanks to C. S. Lewis, J. R. R. Tolkien, Madeleine L'Engle, and others writing from a Christian perspective, some in the Christian community have begun to recover from this impoverishment and to regain an appreciation of the language of myth and symbol.

Jung was particularly exasperated by theologians who refused to recognize what he called "the foundations of religious experience." Despite the empirical evidence, they continued to ignore (or not take into account in their theologizing) *psychic reality*. One theologian suggested that no "alien force" could intervene in human life. This really irritated Jung, for he believed that depth psychology had demonstrated such intervention for half a century. The psyche is far from being a homogenous unit. Whether one speaks of "demons" or "autonomous complexes," the psychic experience remains. Theologians would be better advised to take account, Jung said, "of these psychological facts than to go on 'demythologizing' them with rationalistic explanations that are a hundred years behind the times."[8]

The language of religion, and particularly the language of Christianity, fascinated Jung, and remained his main area of interest on into his later years. In his essay "Transformation Symbolism in the Mass,"[9] Jung called attention to the way in which the chief ritual in Christianity symbolically expressed the necessary steps of psychic transformation in the movement toward wholeness. Furthermore, with his technique of dream interpretation, *amplification*, Jung provided a method by which the symbolic language of Christianity could be approached and appreciated.

Protestants have tended to condemn the Catholic Church for its assimilation of the stories of religious truth in the different cultures into which it has moved (one thinks of Mexico). Jung, however, found this appreciation of symbolic language to be of the essence for vital religion. The reinterpretation of the phoenix myth by the early Church fathers as a reference to Christ, Jung said, was an example not only of the myth's vitality, but also of the vitality of Christianity, which was able to interpret and assimilate the myth. Such reinterpretations help link the present with the ancestral heritage, which is still alive in the unconscious. In recent years, Christianity has demonstrated this kind of vitality as it experienced tremendous growth in central Africa, particularly in its use of drums and African music as part of the language of worship. Religions serve as bridges to the ever-living past, which they make alive and present for us. A religious tradition, if it is to remain alive and vital, must continue to interpret its basic story in the light of the understanding of the day. The spiritual vitality of a religious tradition is maintained, Jung said, "only if each age translates the myth into its own language and makes it an essential content of its view of the world."[10]

On the other hand, one must obviously hold on to the spiritual reality witnessed to in the basic story. In an attempt to be "scientific" Christians have too often thrown out the "baby" with what they recognized as dirty bath water. New Testament Christianity could not remain true to itself in an overly rationalistic, materialistic world view. Jung thought that this had happened in his day.

Myths and rituals have the same two aspects that we noted as characteristic of symbols generally. First, there is the *local* character in all myths and rituals: it is "our" ancestor, etc. The image binds the individual to his or her family's system of historically conditioned sentiments, activities, values, and beliefs. Here the symbol functions as part of a sociological organism. Secondly, there is the quality of leading the individual *beyond*. Time and space are overcome. The individual is disengaged from the local, historical, particular conditions and is led into some kind of ineffable experience. Down through the centuries, this has been the "mystery" of the Mass, the "power" of the Lord's Supper. By whatever name it has been called, Christians have found their communion—their union with God—in this ritual action. The symbolic language of myth and ritual serves as a bridge uniting this world and the other.

With his deep appreciation of symbolic language, Jung offered Christianity a way of recovering for the modern individual its ancient method of worship, developed over the centuries—the sacraments. This perhaps would also heal the centuries-old schism in the Church, for a principal bone of contention between the Protestant reformers and the medieval Church was a proper view of the sacraments. The Catholic position emphasized the *real presence;* the Protestant refused the materialistic distortion—which is to make something less than God, God. Once the true meaning of a symbol (to which Jung and others have pointed) is accepted, neither Catholic nor Protestant should have any difficulty with a dogma of the "real presence."

Jung was greatly concerned over the schism in the Christian community. Part of his "challenge" to Christianity was for it to recognize the depotentiating effect of the schism, and to find a way to reunion. That is why, as he said in a letter in 1944, he had sought to establish facts on which the two sides could unite.[11] The moral and spiritual authority of Christianity was diminished by the divisions in the Christian community, Jung said, as anyone outside the institutional structure could plainly see. Attention to the nature and contents of the necessary language of religion could clear the way for Christianity to be reunited and for it to make the truths it has preserved available to the contemporary world.

Chapter Eleven

THE PROBLEM WITH DOGMA

There is a direct relationship between dogma and personal experience, in Jung's thought, which is not so apparent at first glance. Understanding and coming to terms with the implications of that relationship is both a challenge and an opportunity for Christianity. After examining some of Jung's seemingly contradictory thoughts on dogma, I will try to summarize his position, and then to explore some of the implications of his thought for both Protestantism and Catholicism.

Dogma, creed, and ritual, as Jung saw them, are crystallized forms of someone else's religious experience that have been worked over and refined, usually for centuries. Yet for us today, Jung believed, dogma and church ritual tend to minimize personal religious experience precisely because they *are* symbolic expressions of the unconscious. They "let off steam," so to speak, but without integrating that "steam" into the cooking process. Making use of symbolic language, dogma and ritual perform the necessary function of serving as channels of psychic energy. They provide the "connection" between the archetypes of the unconscious and consciousness, yet, paradoxically, they preclude raising that "connection" into a personal experience that grips the whole person. The symbols are not experienced consciously. When religious experience remains at the level of belief, and even "required belief," it becomes subject to doubt, and does not keep pace with the developing consciousness of the ego (nor of the developing consciousness of the age).

"Dogma," Jung said, "like mythology in general, expresses the quintessence of inner experience and thus formulates the operative principles of . . . the collective unconscious."[1] Whether for better or worse, this approach is no longer generally available. Authoritarian answers are foreign to our present way of thinking. The word *dogma* itself has become odious. No one wants to be accused of being dogmatic. It suggests the rigidity of a prejudice. Even seminaries seldom offer courses in "dogmatic theology" anymore, but prefer to use some other adjective instead. For most people, Jung said, dogma has lost its meaning as a symbol for something that was virtually unknowable and yet an operative fact.

One way of solving the contemporary problem of meaninglessness (which accompanies the rejection of dogma and the loss of a symbol system) would be to borrow from Eastern or non-Christian religions. Many have tried this, but to Jung it was a way of evasion. "It cannot be emphasized enough that we are not Orientals, and that we have an entirely different point of departure in these matters," he wrote.[2] While Indian symbols, for example, formulate the unconscious as well as Christian ones do, Jung said, they do so out of the background of their own spiritual past. The Indian religious system is the distilled essence of several thousand years of human experience *in India*. While this can be instructive, it can never express the past that is stored up within the European. The European departs from his own nature, his collective history and experience, when he imitates the East. The possibilities for his own development would be much better, Jung said, if the European "would remain true to himself and evolve out of his own nature all that the East has brought forth in the course of the millennia."[3] Jung found support for this conclusion in his theory about the development of the collective unconscious.

The civilizing premises for the West have been those of Christianity, Jung said. In some parts of Europe the experience of Christianity goes back less than a thousand years, and for most Europeans there had been an even longer period of polytheism and polydemonism before the coming of Christianity. Only a thin wall separates us from pagan times. By way of illustration, Jung pointed out that the last witch was burned in Europe the year his grandfather was born. Furthermore, even in the twentieth century, barbarism has broken out again. A certain inflexibility of dogma was perhaps a necessary development to hold the line for civilization. A similar rigidity, and even fanaticism, could be seen in the spread of Islam, Jung suggested.[4]

Such "dogmatism" (rigidity) may have been necessary and helpful in the evolution of consciousness, Jung thought. However, in our continued movement toward ever higher levels of consciousness, personal experience becomes the only possible authority.

The problem of making the connection with the unconscious has come to the fore in our day. For us, the bridge from dogma to the inner experience of the individual has broken down. Dogma is either rejected entirely or it is simply "believed" without really letting it penetrate one's daily life. It no longer formulates the truths of inner experience for people. Jung said, "It has become a tenet to be accepted in and for itself, with no basis in any experience that would demonstrate its truth."[5]

Jung's various statements about dogma often leave the reader in a quandary: Is Jung "for it" or "against it"? The apparent contradictions in Jung's position on dogma and ritual are resolved upon closer examination. His position can be understood from the following four points:

1. Dogma does give expression to the archetypes of the unconscious. Those age-old motifs and patterns of human experience and wisdom are enshrined in dogma. For example, the feminine is part of life and of the wholeness of what it means to be human, and when it is not adequately symbolized, the pressure from the unconscious for that expression is so strong that it even overcomes the objections and protestations of theologians who (quite rightly) are seeking to interpret the wisdom of their religious tradition to the rationalistic age in which they live. Thus, despite the lack of biblical support for the idea, we find the Pope in 1950 proclaiming

the dogma of the bodily assumption of Mary into heaven, thereby giving symbolic expression to the feminine. For Jung, this was strong evidence of the power of dogma to give expression to unconscious contents. He never wrote a major book after 1950 that did not mention this or refer to this proclamation.[6]

2. Yet, Jung said, dogma is unintelligible to people in a rationalistic age (a) because rationalism has gone so far as to lose any appreciation of symbolic language in general, and takes as "true" only that which is literal and material; and (b) because the particular symbols used in the expression of the dogma are often no longer a part of contemporary life. For example, the symbol of the "good shepherd" was a part of daily life for a pastoral people and even the chief title of one of the loving deities in a Greek religion before the arrival of Christianity on the scene; however, it becomes of questionable value in an urban culture, where very few people are aware of the requisite qualities of a shepherd.

3. Third, Jung said that even when the symbols are functioning for us, that is, "grasping us in our depths" (and therefore, a "religious experience"), they still function on a more unconscious level than the rising level of consciousness demands. Today people require a more *personal* encounter with the living God if they are to give and commit their daily lives to a continuing relationship with that God. Here I think we can see the "charismatic renewal movement," with its emphasis on the experience of speaking in tongues, as evidence that Jung was at least right in his insistence that the modern person wants to *know*—that is personally experience—and not just *"believe in* the Lord Jesus Christ" (in the customary formula of evangelical Christianity). Interestingly, this movement, at least in the United States, has spread—mostly since Jung's death in 1961—to Catholicism, the home of dogma, and constitutes a surprising percentage of those Catholics remaining active in the Church.

4. Jung thought "only a few" are capable of—or interested in—bearing the strain of the union of opposites as a personal experi-

ence. Jesus' own difficulty with this experience was reflected, he felt, in the story of the temptations—which occurs right after his baptism and acceptance of God's call. Also, St. Paul "went away" for a while after his own conversion experience on the Damascus road—perhaps to integrate his tremendous transcendental religious experience. Paul's extreme persecution of the Christians is perhaps indicative of the exacerbation of the tension of opposites in his psyche just prior to his conversion. Not everyone is prepared to handle an experience of the union of opposites, Jung felt. (One author of the New Testament expressed a similar concern when he wrote, "It is a fearful thing to fall into the hands of the living God." Hebrews 10:31) Presumably, for those unable to venture into a personal experience of the union of opposites (which Jung described as an experience of "grace"), some symbolic system by which a connection with the unconscious can be appropriated (even though not done consciously) is nevertheless needed. Dogma, of course, traditionally fulfilled this role. (Some of Jung's comments about the Church's ability "to move masses" are explored further in chapter 13.)

Thus, in Jung's view, dogma could be useful, but it also diffused and deflected religious experience. Rather than dogma, I think we have to say that the villain for Jung was *institutional religion* as he and his patients had known it. That was a restricting, inhibiting, damaging influence on the individual. He had a kind of psychopathology of religion in his understanding of what he called the "creeds." While institutional religions were originally based upon direct, personal experiences of individuals (such as St. Paul's conversion), they tended in succeeding generations to become a matter of "faith"—that is, as Jung said, "trust or loyalty, faith and confidence in a certain experience of a numinous nature and in the change of consciousness that ensues."[7] The original experience became impersonal, rigid, and unchangeable as it was gradually incorporated into a ritual to be repeated. The "creeds" dissipated the original numinous experience of individuals.

To the extent that one is unconscious of the projections present, that is, to the extent it is really a matter of *credo* (I believe), then to that extent the "creeds" may serve a useful function for the person, that is, may perform an integrative function. Some Jungians speak of letting their patients keep (perhaps even encouraging them to, as Jung taught) their adherence to the Christian myth "as long as they can." The other road is a "difficult" one, it is said. One is reminded at times of some Christians' references to "the deeper walk." Actually, the Jungian psychotherapists feel fairly confident that the patient who walks in their door is Jung's "modern man," for whom the myth of the "creeds" no longer lives. He has "lost his soul," his mediator. He is in search of his own personal myth, his own story, his own restoration to that which gives meaning.

It is personal, individual experience that convinces people today. In the escape from dogma lies the opportunity for the Protestant. As Jung saw it, Protestantism strips away all spiritual safeguards and means of defense against an immediate experience of the forces in the unconscious. He wrote, "The Protestant is left to God alone. For him there is no confession, no absolution, no possibility of an expiatory *opus divinum* of any kind." [8] This tends to produce for the Protestant, Jung thought, a sharper conscience—and hence awareness. On the other hand, for the Catholic, the rites of confession and absolution are always at hand to reduce any excess of tension. Thus the Protestant has a greater chance to become conscious of sin (of separation and dividedness), which would lead him or her to greater self-understanding. A bad conscience, Jung said, can be like a gift from heaven if it is used in the interests of higher self-criticism. Such activity can lead one to see what motives are governing one's actions. It may lead one to become aware of what was previously unconscious. Indeed, such self-examination can open the door to immediate religious experience.

Jung's high regard for the truths expressed in dogma, and his equally high regard for the importance of personal religious experience, are indicated in some remarks he made in a letter he wrote in 1944. Jung said that while he knew little of Catholic doctrine, that little was enough to make it an "inalienable possession" for him. And, at the same time, he said he knew so much about Protestantism that he could never give it up.[9]

In Jung's view, the Protestant has a better opportunity of experiencing *consciously* the task of life—individuation. The Catholic has the advantage of having the road map for this path of individuation laid out for him in the symbols of the dogmas of the Church. On the other hand, the Catholic has the disadvantage of being able to follow this path rather unconsciously, as the walls of dogma "shield" him or her from the pressure toward conscious realization. Nevertheless, Catholic dogma is a better expression of the necessary union of opposites (wholeness) than the theological theories of the Protestant. The latter merely give expression to and formulate the conscious mind alone, Jung said. "Dogma, on the contrary, aptly expresses the living process of the unconscious in the form of the drama of repentance, sacrifice, and redemption."[10]

The process of individuation consciously realized is a difficult one. It is no easy matter to accept oneself just as one is! It requires courage *to be*. The personal experience of this acceptance when formulated in ultimate terms is: God accepts me. Indeed, in the language of the Christian story, God even "died for me." It is the inner realization of this truth that constitutes the essence of the Christian experience—it is the "good news" that dogma and ritual seek to express.

In Jung's view, the ideas in religion are products of a preconscious knowledge that, always and everywhere, expresses itself in symbols. They are universal psychic facts; hence they work, even if the intellect does not grasp them as such. Every development in rational consciousness, however, has tended to lead us further away from the truth of the symbols. We cannot turn the clock back,

Jung said, and force ourselves to believe "what we know is not true"; but we could give some thought to what the symbols really mean and, in that way, recover something of the treasures of our civilization. Recognizing religious truths for what they are, as symbols, opens the door to the wisdom of the past. We can then be grateful to the Church for not only conserving them, but developing them dogmatically. That was why, Jung said, he had undertaken to submit old dogmas to psychological scrutiny. It was not that he felt he knew better than others, but rather that anything which had been held in such high regard for so many centuries must surely be "a valid statement concerning those things which one cannot see with the eyes or touch with the hands."[11]

Thus, for Jung, dogma was something to be appreciated, but also something to move beyond. The task today was to continue the Reformation, to continue to strip away the remaining vestiges of ecclesiasticism that still cling to Protestantism, but to do so cognizant of the wisdom expressed in the symbolism of the dogmas of the Catholic Church. As Jung saw it, the coming pattern of religious experience will be individual, and it will also be Christian in the broadest sense, but not ecclesiastical.

Throughout the Church, in recent years, there have been a number of movements that emphasized a recognition of the importance of *individual* religious experience. One example stands out in my own memory particularly. In 1954, Claxton Monro, the rector of St. Stephen's Episcopal Church in Houston, Texas, proclaimed to his congregation (and later, in numerous conferences across the nation) an insight about the Church for the future which he could only view as God-given. It went something like this:

> The witnessing fellowship of Christian laymen is destined to become, in the decades ahead, the center of authority and power in the Church, and God is going to speak through this witnessing community as He spoke through the Bible at the time of the Protestant Reformation.

While Jung spoke of continuing the Protestant Reformation, in Monro's view, the life of the Church (after the early centuries of the beginning of Christianity) could be divided into three eras: the medieval Church, the age of the Protestant Reformation, and the modern world. The lines of division for each age are indicated by what the "lively" Christians of that age found to be the focus of power and authority for the Christian community. Monro summed up his message in three points: (1) The uneducated individual in medieval society accepted the authority of the institutional Church. (2) The newly awakened minds of the Renaissance accepted the authority of theology based on the Bible. (3) The humanistic, scientific, and pragmatic spirit of this age will accept the authority of experiential, personal encounter with the living God.[12] Christianity spread during the three hundred years that it was illegal in the Roman empire largely by word of mouth. One person told another about his or her personal religious experience. Personal experience could not be doubted. This was precisely the authority to which the contemporary person would also listen, Monro said.

Only limited recognition, or acceptance, of Monro's insight about the centrality of the individual lay person's religious experience has followed on the part of institutional Christianity. However, in the years since Monro first alerted me to the importance of individual religious experience, it has been my observation that wherever one found vitality in the life of the Christian community, one found activities that focused on the individual experience of the Christian. Jung has analyzed, from a psychological perspective, why this is so.

Jung's challenge to Christianity in regard to the necessity for personal experience has been echoed by many voices in addition to Monro's. Jung told us why such personal experiences were important. Symbols produced by the unconscious that were personally experienced, he said, were the one thing capable of convincing the critical mind of today. "They are convincing," he said, "for a very old-fashioned reason: They are *overwhelming*, which is precisely what the Latin word *convincere* means."[13]

Religious experience is subjective and therefore liable to boundless error. Monro found that in tradition-laden and theologically "careful" churches, it takes a brave pastor to permit the people to witness publicly about their encounter with the living God. Such reluctance is understandable, as personal witness about an individual experience may well depart from the creedal position of the local ecclesiastical authority. Institutional Christianity may not have recognized the arrival of Monro's "third age." But the spiritual adventure of our time (as Jung once called it) seems to call for the exposure of human consciousness to "the undefinable." Jung said that we could undertake this challenge, however, at least with some assurance that even in the unconscious there are psychic laws that no individual invented. Further, we could begin to have some knowledge of those laws through a fresh approach to the symbolism of Christian dogma. As the crystallized experience of innumerable individuals over the centuries, dogma gives a more complete picture than any single experience can do of the contours and contents of those psychic laws operative in the collective unconscious. Jung remarked about dogma: "Only heedless fools will wish to destroy this; the lover of the soul, never."[14]

The challenge, as I see it, that Jung's insights about dogma and the necessity of personal religious experience leave us in this: conscious *commitment* is essential. In its freedom and response to the "newness" of life today, the Christian community must not abandon the wisdom and techniques that produced dogma. We need still to *build* vessels and channels for the energy of experience to flow in. Focused attention is still called for. Much of the dynamism of the Pentecostal experience has been dissipated in the older specifically Pentecostal churches, I suspect, because of the lack of commitment to any structure or symbol system. The forms of dogma are absent; there is no container or vessel. On the other hand, the dynamism of the personal experience is almost overwhelming; the power is there. Form and dynamism are a polarity, and an extreme expression of either end of the polarity misses the mark. Structure without the spirit of a personal living experience is useless, as the current Catholic renewal movement is pointing out. On the other hand, the dynamic force of personal experience without some structure in which commitment can find expression does not produce lasting results for the individual or society. The potential energy present in an oil well gusher is not usable until the pipelines are built. Commitment is made possible by combining the power and dynamism of the personal religious experience with the symbolic vessels or forms (preserved in dogma) in which the personal experience can find conscious expression.

Chapter Twelve

THE VOICE OF GOD
CAN STILL BE HEARD!

Vocatus atque non vocatus, Deus aderit (Called and not called, God will be there). This is the inscription carved over the doorway of Jung's house in Kusnacht/Zurich. For him, this was a basic truth of life. For Jung, unlike Freud, God was no "illusion." The experience of "the other" very early and throughout his life was an experience Jung could never doubt. He described the dreams, visions, and voices he experienced throughout his life in his autobiographical *Memories, Dreams, Reflections.* He directed that it not be included in the collected works of his writings, and he forbade its publication until after his death. It was too personal and too uncommon; he did not want to hear what would be said about him when it was published.

Jung's interpretation of these personal experiences is of particular interest to Christians. Even though he always sought to be a scientist and an empiricist, declining to make assertions except on the basis of observable experience, he still was able to talk about God. In a letter written a few years before his death, Jung spoke about his use of the term *God* with respect to his experience of an autonomous agent in the psyche. Such experiences of a will other than one's own and contrary to one's own conscious intentions are not uncommon. Jung said that he knew he was not alone in having such experiences. A question remained, however, which he posed for himself and then answered. "But why call this something 'God'? I would ask: 'Why not?' It has always been called 'God.' An excellent and very suitable name indeed."[1]

Jung objected to the expression *wholly other* with respect to God. He said it was "psychologically quite unthinkable" for God to be considered the "wholly other" when in fact God was "one of the soul's deepest and closest intimacies."[2]

Submission to the "will of God" is the ultimate task involved in the whole process of individuation. Wholeness lies in developing a dialogue between the self (the "God-image" in man) and the ego (the center of conscious willing and striving). In the psychic experience of a conflict that seems irresolvable, when the ego has gone to the end of its wits, then, Jung found, from the unconscious (for those who are engaged in the analytic process of paying attention to the unconscious), a reconciling symbol may appear as a kind of new directive. A new basis for the reconciliation of the opposing forces is given, in symbolic language, and from a center unknown to us.[3]

Christians have tended, in recent centuries, to limit their understanding of "vocation," in the formal sense of speaking about God's "calling," to those who felt called to be clergy or to enter a religious order. The "freeing" experience of following God's will, however, has long been expressed in Christian devotion—for example, in the phrase from the 1928 Book of Common Prayer: "whose service is perfect freedom."[4] Very similar is the comment by a Jungian analyst: "It is by submitting to the will of life, rather than by trying to manipulate it, that freedom is obtained."[5] Jungian psychology can serve to remind Christianity once again of the importance for all Christians of living in this personal relationship to God.

Jung understood God's call to each person as a call to the realization of his or her own wholeness; however, that wholeness is not the same for every person. More than many a psychologist, Jung recognized the uniqueness of each individual. Jung felt that Christians too often misunderstood the proper meaning of "the imitation of Christ." Throughout the course of history, the Christian, rather than pursuing his or her own destined road to wholeness, attempted to imitate the way taken by Jesus, whereas, in Jung's view, Christ should be regarded as "an examplar who dwells in every Christian as his integral personality."[6] A proper understanding of the "imitation of Christ" would be for each individual to pursue his or her own destined road to wholeness, just as Jesus did in becoming the historical Christ. Jung made this suggestion in a lecture to a group of pastors in 1932. He said that while it was not easy to live a life modeled on Christ's, it was even harder to live one's own life as truly as Christ lived his.[7] Yet people today, Jung concluded, are interested in how they can live their own individual lives, however limited they might appear to be. Every form of imitation seems to them deadening and sterile, and so they have rebelled against any force of tradition that would hold them to old ways. In the optimistic mood of the nineteenth and early twentieth centuries, only the new was good.

Now, as the twentieth century draws to a close, one may discern a new appreciation of the old and the traditional. Perhaps it is nostalgia for a time when the answers seemed easier. Still, we need to feel related to something larger than ourselves if we are to find meaning and value in life. Jung felt that with the abandonment of traditional patterns, which had answers for the question of meaning, only a sense of calling or vocation that stemmed from something other than the strivings of our own egos could begin to answer our sense of the meaninglessness of life.

Perhaps the kind of experience Jung knew about and that he knew could give meaning to life is illustrated by what Dag Hammarskjöld, then Secretary General of the United Nations, wrote in his diary about an inner experience a few months before his death in 1961. He said that at some point a question was put. He did not know who or what questioned him, or even when the question was put, nor did he remember answering it. But at some moment he did answer "yes" to someone or something. "From that hour," he wrote, "I was certain that existence is meaningful and that, therefore, my life, in self-surrender, had a goal."[8]

We are free to choose to follow such inner leading, but we cannot dictate *what* that leading will be. The ego must "surrender," as Christian devotion has always known. Similarly, Jung wrote, "We do not *create* 'God,' we *choose* him."⁹ As we have noted, Jung's understanding of the proper imitation of Christ was that we should respond to God's call to us just as the man of Nazareth, Jesus, had responded to his vocation to be the Christ—and, one might add, even as Mary, in response to the announcement of God's will for her, said, "Be it unto me, according to thy word."

Jung made a distinction between the "Jesus of history" and the "Christ of faith," just as some students of the New Testament have done. In his lectures at Yale in 1937, Jung pointed out that the Church regards the life of Christ as both an historical and an eternally existing mystery. This double approach is especially evident in the sacrifice of the Mass. The concrete, personal life of the man from Nazareth has, at the same time, an archetypal character, Jung suggested. Evidence for this can be seen in the numerous parallels between the biographical details and worldwide mythical motifs. Those very connections are what make it so difficult to construct from the gospel accounts an individual life divested of myth. The gospels would, Jung said, "immediately lose their character of wholeness if one tried to separate the individual from the archetypal with a critical scalpel."¹⁰

Jung was particularly impatient with some of the attempts by New Testament scholars to separate the historical from the mythic elements in the New Testament. Writing about one early exponent of biblical "higher criticism," Jung said that such a person talks like that only because he is "no longer impressed by the revelation of holiness and has fallen back on his own mental activity."¹¹ Criticism of that kind, Jung said, always puts on an air of great enlightenment that reminded him of that thick darkness the Word once tried to penetrate with its light. Such critics thought they were dealing with rational facts, whereas "it is and always has been primarily a question of irrational psychic phenomena."¹²

The nonhistorical elements of faith attached themselves to the historical Jesus at a very early date, as is indicated even in the earliest documents in the New Testament. Jung wrote, "He is completely overlaid, or rather smothered, by metaphysical conceptions: he is the ruler over all daemonic forces, the cosmic saviour, the mediating God-man."[13] Elements of religious understanding and images drawn from the interpretation of religious experience from the whole Near Eastern world soon clustered about the human figure. The historical person tended to disappear in the midst of the emotions and projections that swarmed about him. The descriptions we have are based upon what he had become to the community whose religious experience centered upon him. Jung said that the human figure, precisely because of those archetypal projections, had a revelatory effect. He could function in that way because of the unconscious expectations. Jung's understanding of the role of the expectations of the people is perhaps not so far from St. Paul's own more literal comment on the action of the God of history: "But when the fulness of time was come, God sent forth his Son, made of woman, made under the law." (Galatians 4:4) That comment on "when the fulness of time was come" is perhaps not only a reflection of Paul's understanding of Jewish history, but also of his awareness (however unconscious) of the human needs being met in the contemporary religious community.

Jung, however, should not be understood as doubting the person of Jesus. In his last major work, *Mysterium Coniunctionis,* he wrote that while he did not doubt the historical reality of Jesus of Nazareth, he did want to point out that the figure of the Son of Man and of Christ the Redeemer had archetypal antecedents.[14] Earlier, in *Answer to Job,* Jung described how it was possible psychologically for an archetype to take complete possession of a person and to determine his destiny down to the smallest detail. Such occurrences might be accompanied by objective nonpsychic parallel phenomena at the same time. He wrote, "The archetype fulfils itself not only psychically in the individual, but objectively outside the individual. My own conjecture is that Christ was such a personality." [15] It was reflection on this kind of *dual* experience of Jesus as the Christ that led the early Church fathers to produce at the Council of Chalcedon the formula: "One person, with two natures." What Jung meant by the archetypal aspect is what the early Church meant by the divine nature.

Jung's understanding of the human psyche as having a "calling"—that is, as having a "spiritual dimension" as well as an instinctual side—is one way of stating the chief difference of opinion that caused Jung to break with Freud. For Jung, the materials in the depth of the psyche cannot be reduced simply to causes in the personal history of each individual. There is a goal toward which each individual psyche moves. The symbols produced by the unconscious, with their multivalent quality, speak about the future as well as the past. The publishing of these ideas by Jung in 1912 in the book now called *Symbols of Transformation* led to the break with Freud. In this study, Jung called attention to his recognition of the role of symbols and story (myth) in the life of the individual.

In the foreword to the fourth Swiss edition of that book, Jung tells us that he had hardly finished the manuscript when he was struck by what it meant to live with a myth, or what it meant to live without one. The person in our day who thinks he can live without myth is like someone "uprooted." He has no link with the past that lives within, nor even with contemporary society. He lives in a world of his own devising, which he thinks is a newly discovered truth, but which never grips him at any depth. So, Jung said, he was forced to ask himself, "What is the myth you are living?" He found he had no answer to that question, but only "an uncertain cloud of theoretical possibilities." He wondered if there was a "myth" giving order to his own life. To get to know "his myth" became his chief concern, for otherwise, he said, he could not make allowance for his own personal equation in the treatment of his patients. This resolve supported him in his life-long investigation of the subjective contents of the unconscious.[16]

In his autobiography, Jung describes how he finally came to understand and be grasped by a myth that provided for him a meaning for life. Aniela Jaffe, who helped him record and edit his memoirs, says that it is no accident that his "myth of meaning" is recorded there, for Jung did not consider that book a scientific work. The answer to the question of meaning is not a scientific answer, for Jung believed every human interpretation or conjecture to be a confession or a belief.[17] Jung's myth of meaning is a myth of consciousness. He concluded that human history is a story of developing consciousness. Even the Christian message calls for a confrontation of the opposites—a necessary step in the rise of consciousness. What is called for now, Jung felt, is a reconciliation—not of the opposites "God" and "man," as previously understood—but rather of the opposites within the God-image itself. That is what man can do for God—bring consciousness to the creation. Such a goal fits mankind meaningfully into the scheme of creation. It is an explanatory myth that has, Jung said, "slowly taken shape within me in the course of the decades. It is a goal I can acknowledge and esteem, and which therefore satisfies me."[18]

Our myth of meaning, the story we find that tells us who we are, must include some explanation of the meaning of human existence in the cosmos, Jung said; it also must spring from our own experience of psychic wholeness, that is, from the cooperation between the conscious and the unconscious. Again we can see the "two-pronged" characteristic we noted of symbols in general: the concrete (related to us) and the element that leads beyond (that connects us with a larger reality). We cannot create or invent a myth that accomplishes this for us. Rather, it comes to us as a "Word of God," Jung said. We have no way of distinguishing whether it is from God or not. Everything about this Word is known and human, except for the manner in which we are confronted spontaneously and have obligations placed upon us. Our will does not affect the experience, just as we have no explanation for an inspiration. "Our chief feeling about it is that it is not the result of our own ratiocinations, but that it came to us from elsewhere," Jung wrote.[19]

A superficial reading of Jung suggests that he has rejected the plumb line of Christian revelation (Bible and Church)—the crystallized experience of others—and so was left with his subjective feeling of "otherness" as the sole criterion of validity. But such a reading fails to do justice to his concept of archetypes. Jung argued that a distinction should be made as to whether a statement stemmed solely from an isolated subject (that is, with exclusively personal motives), or whether it occurred generally, and stemmed from a collectively present dynamic pattern. In the latter case, that is, when a number of individuals are prompted by an inner impulse to make an identical statement, then it should not be regarded as subjective, but as psychologically objective. Jung's view about the role of dogma in the Church derived from this understanding of archetypal processes, as we saw in the last chapter. What the ego wills is subject to interferences in ways of which the ego is often unaware, Jung said. Practical consideration of archetypal processes to which the ego is subject is what religion is all about, when viewed from a psychological perspective.[20]

Consideration of those processes is the essence of religion for Jung, but many people in the Christian world know nothing about them. Jung said that in his professional work he knew a great many patients—leaving aside pathological hangers-on—who were by no means sickly eccentrics. Rather, he said they were often able, courageous, and upright persons who had repudiated traditional truths for honest and decent reasons, and not from wickedness of heart. All had come to feel that traditional religious truths had somehow become hollow. Either they could not reconcile the scientific and the religious outlooks, or, Jung said, the Christian tenets had lost their authority and their psychological justification.[21]

In my own experience, wherever we find a "living faith" among Christians we find someone who knows personally the "guidance of God" and who has considered the question of "vocation"—of what God is "calling" him or her to do. Jung might say they have found a personal myth. Most of the branches of Christendom that seem to be growing in numbers today are those that speak of God's calling and God's guidance—not those necessarily that have rational and "theologically sound" arguments to present.

There has been a tendency on the part of some to limit the Christian message to what has been called the "social gospel," perhaps partly because it cannot be questioned from a rational perspective, and also, of course, because such a message has been so needed in our contemporary society. Certainly the Christian message includes the "social gospel," but when the personal experience of religion is ignored, the people fall away.

Even Freud noted the necessity for personal religious experience. He was confident that religion could not stand the critical appraisal of "science" (by which he meant psychoanalysis). Religion was simply contrary to reason and to experience, and so, in the end, would have to give way. Freud recognized that religious ideas might be "purified" by restricting them to a belief in a God "whose purposes cannot be discerned" and whose qualities were indefinable. In such a case, Freud said, "they will be proof against the challenge of science; but then they will also lose their hold on human interest." [22]

Freud was right, to a limited extent, and with respect to his prediction of a loss of interest, for that is what has happened to many people—Jung's patients, for example. Many Christian leaders, in their attempt to be intellectual and "scientific," tended to omit any teaching on personal vocation or experiences of God's guidance. The response was, as Freud predicted, a loss of interest. Jung's own confession is to the point: "Only that which acts upon me do I recognize as real and actual. But that which has no effect upon me might as well not exist." [23]

Jung presents Christianity with a challenge: to meditate more deeply on the meaning of vocation, of God's "calling" of each of us. God "calls" each person to realize in his or her exterior life some congruency with that "inner necessity" that can be experienced interiorly if one but knows to "listen," and does so. In Dag Hammarskjöld's experience, it was a matter of saying "yes" to that inner voice. In the last two decades, in the larger denominations of the Church, there has been a growing awareness of renewal movements that focus on the phenomenon of God's guidance, of God's "calling" of each individual. For many, God has become a personal experience, even as Jung said he must be if he is to have any reality for the person.

Most of the staid, established, and traditional branches of the Church have become aware of the challenge presented to them by renewal movements that focus on personal experience—especially by the "charismatic" movement, with its emphasis on a personal, direct encounter with God. But now, from a totally different quarter comes a similar challenge: namely, Jung's observations on the vital, indeed essential, role of personal religious experience—whether encountered in a traditional religious institution or not. The charismatic and renewal movements can find support for their position in Jung's analysis of the psychology of religion. However, those involved in such movements need no "support" from outside for their experience of an encounter with the living Lord. They "know" (as Jung once said he did), and so they don't need to "believe" on the basis of what others say. For the rest of Christendom, the challenge remains—not only to recover the individual experience of the voice of God, and to allow some room for it in its institutional life, but to incorporate in its theology and teaching some understanding of the psychic reality of an inner voice. What Jung has done is to point out to Christianity that its "science" is out of date. The mechanistic world view of the physical sciences of the nineteenth century (and much of the social sciences of the twentieth century) can no longer be thought to accommodate all the available data. There is such a thing as psychic reality. Once this fact is realized, the description of personal experiences such as those to be found in the New Testament no longer strikes the modern ear as something utterly foreign. "Honest to God" incredulity can shift to "honest to God" experience.

During his lifetime Jung saw little evidence of any such vitality in the life of the Christian community. In a letter he wrote a few months before his death in 1961, he spoke of how rare it was for a Christian congregation to hear the fact that the voice of God could still be heard—if one was only humble enough.[24] Jung's challenge to Christianity with respect to listening to the voice of God reminds me of an old Hasidic tale. "Rabbi, why do not people hear the voice of God anymore?" To which the Rabbi replied, "Nowadays, no one will stoop so low."

Chapter Thirteen

GROUPS: HARMFUL OR HELPFUL?

Jung's attitude toward the Christian Church was ambivalent for a number of reasons. Undoubtedly, some of his negative feeling came from his own personal experiences. For one thing, the Church (to which his father had given his life as a pastor), failed to provide a source of strength and healing for his father. In his memoirs, Jung wrote of his early irritation with the Church (during his "student years") because of its failure to meet his father's needs. Jung records that once he overheard his father struggling desperately in a prayer to keep his faith. Jung said he himself was shaken and outraged at once, because he saw how hopelessly his father was entrapped in "theological thinking." The Church, he said, had blocked all avenues by which his father might have reached God directly.[1] Jung also described his thoughts on the occasion, at the age of fifteen, of his own "first Communion," for which he felt he had prepared so carefully. He asked himself, "What was the purpose of this wretched memorial service with the flat bread and the sour wine?"[2] He had expected, apparently, an encounter with God's presence, but had instead experienced only absence. He resolved not to participate in the ceremony again.

In Jung's personal experience, God was very much something to be reckoned with, but he was not to be found in institutional Christianity. Jung said that his father never chastized him for cutting church, which he did as often as possible, nor for not going to Communion. The farther away from the Church he was, Jung said, the better he felt. He missed the organ and the choral music, but certainly not the "religious community." The "worldly" folk seemed to Jung to be far more of a community than the habitual churchgoers. "They were much nicer people, with natural emotions, more sociable and cheerful, warmer-hearted and more sincere."[3] Jung is speaking here of his experience in the late nineteenth century in Europe.

On the other hand, in the course of a lifetime as a psychotherapist, Jung came to appreciate not only the role of religion in the life of an individual, but also the place of the Church. The world's great religions were the world's great psychotherapeutic symbol systems. Among these, Christianity in particular, it seemed to him, had served the function of promoting the development of human consciousness by helping us control our instincts. To be able to leash the pagan drives present in the last days of the Roman Empire, the early Church, as an institution, had to develop in the way it did, Jung thought. The people of that age were ready for the founding of a community based on the idea of loving one another. Inner psychological necessity made the time ripe for such a religion. Humanity does not thrive in a state of licentiousness, Jung said, and both Christianity and its rival religion, Mithraism, provided a moral subjugation of the animal instincts. The feeling of redemption which both religions provided was something we today can scarcely appreciate. "We can," Jung said, "hardly realize the whirlwinds of brutality and unchained libido that roared through the streets of Imperial Rome."[4]

Even the Communion service, which in Jung's own early experience had been so dreadfully inadequate, later came to be understood by him as a ritual beautifully expressing in its symbolism the necessary steps for the soul's development. He described this in a major essay entitled "Transformation Symbolism in the Mass."[5] Jung's appreciation of the function of Church dogma and ritual as carriers and symbolic expressions of religious experience has already been noted.

In a letter in 1945 (when he was 70), Jung spoke of the danger to civilization of the development of the atomic bomb. The possibility, and even probability, of our destroying ourselves seemed obvious and imminent. The only hope, he said, was for some kind of universal retreat from this direction. Only a religious, world-embracing movement was capable of intercepting the seemingly diabolical impulse toward destruction. That was the reason, Jung said, that the question of the Church gripped him so urgently. The Church was probably the one authority in the world able to move the brute masses in a helpful way. If it were able thus to save mankind, Jung said, the Church would have its "reason for being."[6] The Church just might be able to accomplish that task, Jung said, because in decisive moments behavior is not guided by reason, but rather by overpowering unconscious impulses. The symbolism of the Church provided a channel or vessel for receiving and containing the psychic forces of the unconscious.

Another reason for Jung's opposition to the Church, aside from his own negative experience as a youngster, was the fact that the Church was a collectivity, and thus aroused Jung's basic opposition to all collectivities. The basis for Jung's antagonism to collectivities lay in his confidence that they always resulted in a *lowering of consciousness*. Since he considered the highest goal for mankind to be the development of consciousness—and indeed understood it to be a "divine" purpose in the sense that it seemed to be a "given" in the evolutionary story of mankind—he very naturally opposed any hindrance to that development.

For Jung, the larger the group, the more the individuals in that group tend to function as a collective entity.[7] Thus, the larger the group, the more danger there is that individual consciousness will be lost. Curiously enough, Jung said, the Church—whose very task is the care of the individual soul—also tries to make use of mass action. Yet society cannot be regenerated in its spirit unless the individual is regenerated, Jung said, for society is simply the sum total of individuals.[8]

Jung considered the Church to stand for traditional and collective convictions that for many of its members were no longer matters of their own inner experience, but were simply based on "un-reflecting belief." Such belief, he said, is notoriously apt to disappear whenever one starts thinking about it. "Belief," he insisted, "is no adequate substitute for inner experience."[9] Again, in some correspondence rather late in his life, Jung said, "Nothing shields you better against the solitude and forlornness of the divine experience than community. It is the best and safest substitute for individual responsibility."[10]

In Jung's view, collectivities produce mass-mindedness, as modern history (for example, Nazism) demonstrates. Religion (understood as personal experience) can be a "counterbalance" to mass-mindedness. Thus, all political movements that seek to make the state sovereign try to cut the ground from under religion. Religion prevents the state from becoming sovereign because religion involves a dependence on and submission to certain irrational facts of experience. With such religious dependence, the individual is less likely to become wholly dependent on the state. "The individual who is not anchored in God can offer no resistance on his own resources to the physical and moral blandishments of the world," Jung said.[11]

One cannot live without some external point of reference, some giver of meaning, and the danger is that the state is only too ready to provide this. Totalitarian states oppose religion because it provides the individual with an outside point of reference. The religious person can evaluate the state's goals from this independent position. (Even if the state is not deified, Jung warned, other obsessive factors tend to arise, such as money, work, or political influence. He wrote, "You can take away a man's gods, but only to give him others in return.")[12]

While Jung found religion to be a counterbalance to mass-mindedness, he nevertheless saw the Church as tending itself to promote mass-mindedness. He suspected any group of lowering the level of consciousness, upon which everything depended. He wrote in a letter, "I have never found a community which would allow 'full expression to the individual within it.' "[13]

Whenever Jung was critical of the Church because it did not promote individual religious experience, he used the disdainful term *creed*. He wrote, "A creed gives expression to a definite collective belief, whereas the word *religion* expresses a subjective relationship to certain metaphysical, extramundane factors."[14] To Jung, a *creed* is directed to the world at large, whereas the purpose of *religion* is to relate the individual to something beyond (to God in the biblical religions, or, as in Buddhism, to the path of liberation). A *creed* describes the beliefs asserted by the established Church, which includes in its membership vast numbers of people who can only be described as "indifferent" in matters of religion. They are often there simply by force of habit. Perhaps something of Calvin's teaching on the "invisible Church" is reflected in Jung's distinction.

In Jung's view, while the Church has preserved the symbols of transformation, and has promoted the development of consciousness, this has, necessarily, meant compromising with "mundane reality." "Religion" is no longer present, and "faith" disappears when confronted with doubt. In his dissatisfaction with the institutional Church, the individual today is, Jung said, "on the point of losing the life-preserving myth of the inner man which Christianity has treasured up for him."[15] (Jung's interest in this "myth of the inner man," which he felt contained the seeds of renewal, if only the Church would set about the task of reinterpretation, is discussed further in chapter 16.)

I have called Jung's attitude toward the Church ambivalent. However, from Jung's perspective, the balance seems to weigh heavier on the negative side, for although he found several positive things to say about the Church, his approval was never unqualified.

On the positive side, Jung said that: (1) the Church does provide in its symbol system the necessary steps for psychic development (although they are not being personally experienced); (2) the Church is capable of moving masses of people, and such a force is needed to prevent the world's self-destruction (although the Church needs to update its language and understanding to reach the people of today); and (3) the Church is a force against mass-mindedness and the totalitarian state, since the Church's message calls for an individual response (but again, the focus of the institutional Church is not on the individual).

On the negative side, Jung said that: (1) the Church fails to provide personal religious experience (for his father, himself, and his patients, for example) and (2) the Church, like all collectivities, tends to lower consciousness (and thus moves against the goal of mankind). Is Jung right on these last two points?

Obviously, for many, the Church is "dead." God as a personal experience of the individual is absent. For many others, however, and especially since Jung's death in 1961, the "religious community" itself (here and there) has made possible personal religious experience. The widespread interest in Church renewal, from the liturgical *aggiornamento* of Pope John to the neopentecostal movements of both Catholicism and Protestantism, is evidence that all is not dead. The pentecostal experience of the living God is an *experience*, not a "belief" (as discussed in the last chapter).

The kind of experience, however, that Jung felt was so crucial for us today is one that involves, as we have seen, the coming together of both the irrational and reason. To find the one should not lead to a denial of the other—that is Jung's whole point both about what *has* happened (the one-sided development of reason) and what "needs" to happen (the recovery of a recognition of the irrational). Quite often, however, in the neopentecostal movement, the pentecostal experience leads to the adoption of the unreflecting, literalistic, nonsymbolic theology of the "old line" Pentecostal churches.

For example, one aspect of the literalistic approach to the New

Testament that has reappeared in some churches involved in the renewal movement has been an emphasis on St. Paul's first-century notions about women and their subservience to men. This hardly seems to be the essence of the Christian "good news" of God's forgiveness and acceptance of all people, but rather an attempt by Paul to make his congregations "respectable" and in conformity with both the Jewish synagogues and Greek society with respect to the role of women. (This kind of "compromise" with the worldly point of view, occurring even in the early Church, is what Jung objected to so strenuously and what led him to call institutional expressions of the Church *creeds*.) To consider the place and role of women in the light of the social problems of another century is, in religious language, to limit God's guidance of his people to one period of history. Or, in Jung's language, it is to disregard the apparent purpose of creation: the development of consciousness.

Both Catholicism and some branches of Protestantism are facing the question of the ordination of women as clergy. The depths of feeling of whether one is "acceptable" in an ultimate sense (as discussed in chapter 9) is indicated by the remark one woman was heard to make after her particular denomination had voted to approve the ordination of women. She said, with a note of surprise in her voice, "Now I feel *clean!*" (I think Jung would see the feminist T-shirts of our day—"Trust in God, She will provide"—as an outer expression of a corrective movement in the collective unconscious heralded symbolically a quarter of a century earlier by the Pope's 1950 proclamation of the bodily assumption of Mary into heaven.)

During most of this century, the people talking about personally "knowing" God (and not just "believing in him") were largely groups who regarded the study of anything other than the Bible as extraneous, if indeed not of the Devil. It is not surprising, therefore, that there has been a tendency for many in the neopentecostal movement to adopt ideas (such as a literalistic reading of the Bible) from their brethren in the fundamentalist Pentecostal churches, because their own denominations are unreceptive to their personal experience of the living God. When this kind of borrowing occurs, you still have the conflict between faith (that stems from personal experience) and the knowledge that science offers.

Jung's insistence on the necessity of personal, individual experience is borne out by the growth—one might even say recovery—of this kind of emphasis in both Catholicism and Protestantism. One has only to think of the cursillo movement, "Faith at Work," marriage encounter groups, the charismatic renewal, "Faith Alive," Schools of Pastoral Care, and other such developments to see how widespread this emphasis has become. Even liturgical renewal (for example, the changes coming out of Vatican II and the revisions of the Book of Common Prayer) focuses on meaningful individual participation.

I would say that Jung was correct in faulting the Christian Church for its lack of attention in the past to personal religious experience. However, the situation now is not quite the same as it was when Jung was writing; Church renewal with this kind of emphasis *is* underway. The danger today is that many such movements, which focus on personal experience, have adopted an out-of-date world view. Christianity is faced with the challenge now of bringing its theology and teaching into accord with the experience of its people. The recognition by the institution of the essential language of religion (as discussed in chapter 10) is necessary today.

On Jung's second charge, that the Church (like all collectivities) tends to lower consciousness, I suggest that the opposite is also true. (Jung himself once said, I believe, that if a statement is true from a psychological perspective, the opposite is also true.) I would argue that a group or collectivity of some kind is necessary for individual religious experience to be possible.

In speaking about individual religious experience, Jung once pointed out to a group of pastors that experiences simply happen;

they cannot be *made*. Their independence of our activity, however, is not absolute, but relative. "We can draw closer to them—that much lies within our human reach."[16] Jung cautioned, however, against calling the ways that bring us nearer to living experience "methods," for the very word has a deadening effect. Furthermore, Jung reminded the pastors, the way to personal religious experience is a venture that requires total commitment.

But how do you "draw near"? Is not at least one other person needed—someone or a group to hold out the possibility of renewal, of transformation? Personal witnessing has always been the means of evangelization, whether it is the testimony of a Hindu *Hari Krishna* chanter, the testimony of someone who has "found Jesus," or the testimony of someone who has found a meaning in life through the processes of Jungian "soul healing." In his memoirs, Jung said that only the doctors who know how to cope with themselves and their own problems will be able to teach patients to do the same. "The doctor is effective only when he himself is affected. 'Only the wounded physician heals.' "[17]

"To draw near," two things seem to be needed. First, one has to hear about the possibility of such an experience. And second, one has to be given the means of interpreting what has happened before the experience can be integrative. Providing the imagery for the individual's world view has always been the function of a group, of a religious community. Studies in the field of "sociology of knowledge" have shown us how this is necessarily so.[18]

You can take away someone's church, to paraphrase Jung, but don't you end up providing another? In response to a request by the Analytical Psychology Club of New York to comment on the positive values to the individual of participation in a group, Jung seems to have been reluctant to do so. Nevertheless, in a letter in 1948, after issuing a warning against the dangers of an individual identifying with a collectivity, he commented on some positive features of groups. For one thing, he said, a positive relationship between an individual and society or a group is essential, for no individual stands alone. Furthermore, the very center of an individual, the *self*, is of a conglomerate nature. He wrote, "It is, as it were, a group. It is a collectivity in itself and therefore always, when it works most positively, creates a group."[19] That was the reason, he went on to say, for the existence of the New York Club. As if to prove his point, in the years since Jung made that comment, discussion groups and lecture societies devoted to his thought have arisen in most major cities.

Jung experimented with group meetings through the Psychology Club in Zurich. Several of his friends and colleagues in recent years have written warmly of their memories of the early days of that club. Jung, however, remained skeptical of the value of groups, and following his lead, most Jungian analysts were suspicious of group therapy. After Jung's death, however, a number of Jungians began to call attention to positive values in the group therapy experience. In a 1964 issue of *The Journal of Analytical Psychology*, Edward Whitmont wrote about his reasons for giving group therapy a try. In addition to the requests and inquiries of some of his patients, he said, he could not ignore the fact that "the great religions always had given special value to group worship as a necessary complement to the individual encounter with the numinous."[20] This fact suggested that there might be a specific therapeutic dimension contained in the group experience. Such a "group archetype" could cause trouble if ignored, but could be of constructive help if adequately confronted and related to, he concluded.

Group therapists have found that for many something gets accomplished in group sessions that would not have occurred in individual sessions with the analyst, or at least would have taken much longer. There can be a *raising* of consciousness in a group.

Obviously Jung is right when he claims that consciousness can be lowered by participation in a group. That mobs carry out lynchings is an easy example. On the other hand, murder is also committed by lonely individuals, sometimes with premeditation and sometimes in the heat of passion. Furthermore, *isolation* is one technique (among others) used in brainwashing, and it results in a *lowering* of consciousness. On the other hand, the techniques of "brainstorming" and "think tanks" suggest that consciousness may also be *raised* by participation in groups.

Finally, the question remains: how *individual* is the individual experience that Jung quite rightly prizes? All experience is *interpreted experience*. For example, if we hear a loud noise, we immediately form some tentative hypotheses as to what it was, based on our previous personal experience or other experiences we have read or heard about: an airplane sped through the sound barrier, the cat knocked over a vase, and so on. That which doesn't fit any categories at hand becomes the uncanny—sometimes both fascinating and terrifying.

We are all aware that to grow into a human being, we must be reared by humans. People are made by people. However, it has not been so clear to most of us how far-reaching this proposition is. The relatively new discipline of the sociology of knowledge tells us that what we find plausible, that is, believable, with respect to reality depends upon the social support these ideas receive. We get our ideas about the world originally from other human beings, and these continue to be plausible to us largely because they continue to be affirmed by others. We need a social support group. We may find the support in books instead of immediate associations, but our world view is mediated to us. Even the most original of thinkers has had bits and pieces of his or her constructs mediated from others.

In his Gifford Lectures, *Nature, Man and God*, William Temple (later Archbishop of Canterbury) made the point that any private experience of a revelatory character requires *the coincidence of event and appreciation* (of the event). The appreciation of the event does not have to be contemporaneous with the event, he said, but until it is present, the event, though revelatory in its own character, is not yet fully revelation. He wrote, "If no one had recognized

Christ, the Incarnation would have occurred, but it would have failed to affect a revelation of God."[21]

One of the functions all religious communities serve is providing the imagery and language for "appreciating the event"—for knowing what has happened. Personal religious experience is primary. It is, as Jung said, what is convincing. But, Temple pointed out, the interpretation of the experience is a necessary concomitant. The dogmas and doctrines of the Church provide the guidelines for interpretation. In Temple's view, faith is not the holding of correct doctrines, but rather a personal fellowship with the living God. Correct doctrine, he said, will express this encounter, assist it, and issue from it. Furthermore, incorrect doctrine will misrepresent the encounter and hinder or prevent it. The place of doctrine, however, is still secondary, not primary. Temple wrote, "What is offered to man's apprehension in any specific Revelation is not truth concerning God but the living God Himself."[22] That was precisely Jung's point.

The question arises, however, whether Jung himself recognized the implications of Temple's point. As we have noted earlier, Jung's techniques for "appreciation" are those of personal and general *amplification*. No one religious tradition provides the imagery or language for this process of appropriating the raw data of the experience (of the unconscious), but all are taken together—all the products of human experience from the whole of human history. The process of sifting and the "acceptance" of the interpretation is left to the analysand (or patient), whose primary experience it is. However, the presence of a mediating community seems clear. The world view of the analyst is a most significant factor. Value decisions are implicit in the amplifications, whether recognized or not. It is dangerous when this is ignored by Jungian analysts, who, following Jung, may tend "to leave ethics to the theologians."

The question also arises whether many Christians recognize the implications of Temple's point. They are ready to affirm their personal encounter with God, but see no need for the institutional

Church that provided them with the tools for "appreciating the event." Some sense of community, however, is inevitable and essential. In his devotional book *Readings in St. John's Gospel,* Temple warned Christians that even in their personal encounter with God a mediating community is always present.[23]

We are social animals; we need to feel that we are not entirely alone in our seemingly unique experiences. Sanity is socially defined, as Jung said. Jung told us something of the sense of relief he felt when he realized that there had been others who had had experiences like his—the early Church fathers, the gnostics, the alchemists, and still others, in non-European cultures. Jung wrote, "That which is *only* individual has an isolating effect and the sick person will never be healed by becoming a mere individualist."[24]

Whether groups have a constructive or destructive effect on the individual perhaps depends upon the nature of the meeting. In her book *Knowing Woman,* Irene Clarement de Castillejo, a Jungian analyst, has given us a clue to understanding the difference in the effect groups have with her concept of *meeting.* Meeting does not take place between people when one or both hide behind screens, she says. We can go for days or months without really meeting anyone, even though we are with people all day. Husbands and wives may have the closest physical intimacy for years and yet have no real meeting. Each is wrapped away in isolation. She writes, "For there to be a meeting, it seems as though a third, a something else, is always present."[25] That "third" may be called Love or the Holy Spirit, she adds. Jungians would perhaps speak of it as a constellation of the *self.*

The presence of the "Other" is, of course, well known in the small-group movement in Christianity, but perhaps it is not so well known (among Christians) that this phenomenon also occurs *extra ecclesiam,* as Jung would say—outside the Church. On the other hand, the possibility of a "group archetype" (the fact that there are positive group experiences, a "raising" of consciousness) is something Jungians will have to come to terms with in their evaluation of institutional Christianity. Furthermore, both Jungians and others who cherish individual religious experiences need to recognize the fact that there is, inevitably, for all personal experiences, a mediation or interpretation provided by a community of some kind. Community involves a "uniting with." It is, however, not only a unity with each other, but involves an inner unity with de Castillejo's "third"—with the source of our being—with the Creator—with the One in whom we live and move and have our being. Perhaps the basic challenge to Christianity posed by Jung's observations about the group experience is this: the *reality* of God and of our inner experience of God must never be lost in our experience of groups and community.

Chapter Fourteen

EVIL AS THE
"DARK SIDE" OF GOD

Jung challenged Christianity most sharply with his theory (practically a dogma for his close associates) of the "dark side" of God. Characteristically, he turned to the early Church fathers for support. Jung wrote, "Clement of Rome taught that God rules the world with a right and a left hand, the right Christ, the left Satan."[1] As the opposites are united in one God, Clement's view is clearly monotheistic; however, Jung said, later Christianity is dualistic, inasmuch as one half of the opposites (personified in Satan) are split off. God is *only* good. For Christianity to claim to be a monotheism, Jung argued, it is necessary to assume the opposites as being contained in God. This was the gauntlet Jung threw down at the feet of the Christian community late in his life in the book *Answer to Job.* His theories had been developing all his life—ever since his experience of a "counter-will" as a twelve-year-old boy.[2]

Jung said that he did not pose this challenge until late in life because he knew the trouble it would cause and the danger of being misunderstood. In the preface to his book, Jung described the urgency with which the subject gripped him. He decided to write the book despite his hesitations, and to write it in the form of describing a personal experience, carried, as he said, "by subjective emotions." He wrote, "I deliberately chose this form because I wanted to avoid the impression that I had any idea of announcing an 'eternal truth.' "[3] Jung said that his book did not purport to be anything but the voice or question of one individual who, nevertheless, hoped to meet with thoughtfulness on the part of the public.

Jung always said that he spoke of what could be known, that is, of the processes and images in the psyche—not of metaphysical or "eternal truths." However, he also told us that it was important to write *Answer to Job*, because our metaphysical formulae are not only puzzling, but misleading. The understanding of God as all good is not possible for people today, Jung felt, and this "impossibility" has often meant throwing out the baby (the reality of God) with the bath water (the traditional formulae, which see God as all good). This abandonment of God has had some unfortunate results: among them, a mechanistic view of the universe, an absence of any appreciation of the spiritual, and a false picture of reality—not to mention a problem of meaninglessness. While Jung may not have been announcing an eternal truth, he was at least suggesting a possible alternative viewpoint, about which he was himself quite confident and that he felt to be salvific for at least a number of people.

The view that God is responsible for (if he does not indeed "send") evil has commended itself to many. Christians who share this view generally assume that it is "good" for us in some way we do not understand. Jung, however, went a step further; he suggested that the "archetype of wholeness" that lies in back of what have been called "God experiences" encompasses both good and evil—is, as Nietzsche said, "beyond good and evil."

The challenge Jung posed to the Christian community in this area was for it to provide some definite answer to the mystery of the presence of evil in the world—an answer that could be understood by the average person, whether in the church pew or in Jung's consulting office. The problem of evil can be stated in this way: If God is all powerful and also good, then why is there evil in the world? How can a good God allow it? The answer of many contemporary people was summarized by a character in Archibald MacLeish's play *J.B.*: "If God is God he is not good. If God is good He is not God."[4] Suggested Christian answers (known technically as *theodicies*) usually qualify the "all-powerful"—for example, that for the sake of allowing free choice in his creation (necessary for there to be love) God gives up some of his power. In his answer, Jung opted for the other alternative—namely, that God is only about three-quarters good.

If the Judeo-Christian tradition offers no easily understood answer to the problem of evil, the great religious traditions of India, on the other hand, have a neat solution. The doctrine of *karma* provides an explanation: unmerited suffering in this life is the consequence of evil choices made in an earlier life. The "law of retribution" certainly satisfies the demands of justice. Jung suggested an answer to the problem of evil with his teaching on the "dark side" of God.

Jung's answer was no hasty one, as he himself told us. It was the result of a lifelong wrestling with the problem in his own experiences and those of his patients. A review and elaboration of some of Jung's basic ideas about the psyche suggest how he arrived at the theory that God has a dark side. As noted earlier, Jung encountered in his investigations of psychic experience what he came to call the *self*. The self is a symbol of totality, a center of power and authority in the psyche that is over and beyond the ego, the center of consciousness—hence, it might well be called, he said, the "God-image" in the psyche. The psyche encompasses more than consciousness, for it includes the matrix out of which consciousness develops. Furthermore, there is a push toward a particular development in each individual that seems to come from this larger psyche, from beyond the center of consciousness, from beyond the conscious willing and striving of the ego. This "counter-will" is often at cross purposes with the will of the ego, yet when followed or "obeyed" seems to lead to a new center of integration and peace—the kind of experience one would expect when one has been obedient to "God's will," as traditionally understood.

The steps along the path of integration (the process of individuation) involve, as we have noted, a reintegration of that which has been differentiated out into consciousness, that is, an awareness the contents of one's unconscious. Since consciousness involves the separation of opposites, a polarity is necessarily developed. Recognition of the *shadow*, and its assimilation, is generally the first task in the process of individuation, Jung said. This "dark side" of the psyche is not necessarily evil, but it does include that which has been rejected consciously. It includes all those "roads not taken."

The symbols of wholeness that Jung found most often portrayed in the unconscious involve a union of opposites, and, further, the union of two sets of opposites, or a quaternity. The number *four* is the symbol of wholeness, Jung decided, and he cited examples from all the world's mythologies and religions as evidence, in addition to the dreams of his patients. *Threes* occur in symbolism, but they are evidence of incompleteness, and *fives* are an indication of an imbalance and a lack of resolution. These conclusions led Jung to question the symbol of the Trinity as a symbol for God. It is incomplete, he felt, because the *fourth* is missing.[5]

In one way, Jung said, it is the feminine that is missing. The objective psyche (the collective unconscious) pushes us toward a recognition of wholeness, and hence the missing feminine. Jung saw the proclamation by the Pope in 1950 of the dogma of the bodily assumption of Mary into heaven as an example of popular pressure demanding the recognition of the feminine. It was a psychic need. After several centuries of popular devotion along this line, the Pope responded with his declaration, despite the rationalistic objections of twentieth-century Roman Catholic theologians. In Jung's view, the collective unconscious had asserted a corrective in the dominant symbol of wholeness.

Jung wrote, "The Protestant standpoint has lost ground by not understanding the signs of the times and by ignoring the continued operation of the Holy Ghost."[6] In Jung's view, Protestants were not only out of touch with the archetypal happenings in the psyche of the individual and that of the masses, they seemed to be closing the door to any further guidance by the Holy Spirit. The proclamation of the dogma of the Assumption, Jung said, left Protestantism with the odium of being nothing but a man's religion, as no metaphysical representation of woman was present in its symbolism. "Protestantism has obviously not given sufficient attention to the signs of the times which point to the equality of women."[7] The "liberation theology" of recent years supports Jung's point. Many branches of Protestantism, of course, have "given equality" to women by allowing their ordination.

In other Trinity/Quaternity discussions, Jung spoke of the missing *fourth* as the principle of evil, personified as Satan. The casual reader might conclude from these various and varying references to the fourth principle that Jung equated Mary (the feminine) with Satan (evil), since each is at times presented as the missing "fourth" of the Trinity. But although it is fair to say that Jung was careless at times, he was not such a male chauvinist as that. Such seeming inconsistencies arise because he took whatever the occasion provided as an opportunity to point out the inadequacy of the Trinity as a symbol for God. The polarities of good/evil and masculine/feminine are major ones as experienced in daily life. In Jung's view, any symbol of wholeness should encompass both.

Jung's primary basis for concluding that God is a union of opposites is that the psyche's God-experiences involve a union of opposites (as discussed in chapter 9). In the psyche's experience of the process of individuation, both the shadow and the anima or animus (contrasexual side) must be integrated. The reconciling symbols (whether in outer action or inner images) that accomplish this integration, as experienced by Jung and his patients, are symbols of wholeness that encompass both sides of the polarities. Furthermore, if one continues in the "dialogue" between the conscious and the unconscious, Jung observed, one may encounter a symbol of the self. Symbols of the self express both sides of all the polarities of existence. Particular images or symbols in an individual's experience may focus on one polarity rather than another. However, inasmuch as such symbols have a uniting, reconciling quality, they belong to the same family of salvific experiences. The person experiences an inner healing of that sense of dividedness that had been the psyche's condition prior to the experience.

It would be presumptuous to question Jung's clinical observations about the experiences of the psyche. I, for one, would not do so. It is Jung, above all, who has taught us that to be human is to be the creature *par excellence* caught in the tension of opposites. This is the price we pay for being that part of nature that has become conscious of itself. Consciousness means awareness—awareness of a choice to be made. The tension of opposites is inescapable. This is the *experience of the psyche*, which Jung has so imaginatively charted for us. But, one may ask, need we assume that this particular experience of the psyche describes the character of God? We are split, divided entities, but is God necessarily so? Isn't that possibly just another anthropomorphic projection?

It may be that Jung himself was never able to withdraw the projection of evil as such—that is, to express it in ultimate terms, to withdraw the projection of evil upon God.[8] *Answer to Job*, which he wrote in his late seventies, has unmistakable emotional overtones, to which Jung himself called attention in his introduction. And, it is *affect*, as Jung said, which is the clue to the presence of a projection. The gaps in our knowledge are filled in with projections; surely it is the mystery of evil that is the great unknown in Christianity.

The encounter with the self that the psyche experiences entails a reconciliation of those opposites that have been at war in the psyche, but it seems questionable to suppose that this necessarily means that what is encountered by "beyond" (from, or *via*, the collective unconscious) has the same character. Not all personal experiences are in accord with those of Jung and his patients. The fact that for so many in the Church through the centuries God *has* been a matter of experience and not just belief, and that the experience has been perceived as an encounter with the God of Love provides a basis for questioning Jung's conclusion. My personal experience of the Christian story leads me to do so. My own encounter with that "Love which will not let me go" says that in the depths of the mystery of life, love is the ultimate reality. Jung's personal experience of the God Abraxas (described in his "Seven Sermons to the Dead," found as Appendix V in some editions of *Memories, Dreams, Reflections*), obviously tells him otherwise. One cannot, as Jung said, argue with experience. One can only seek to live out the implications of what one "knows."

It is also true, as Jung has said, that we cannot necessarily assume that what is experienced in the psyche tells us any metaphysical truths. As William James said about religious experiences in the mystical tradition, "That region contains every kind of matter: 'seraph and snake' abide there side by side. To come from thence is no infallible credential."[9] In most of his writing, Jung managed to avoid moving outside the sphere of the empiricist. Here, in such a crucial area of life, he could not resist suggesting a conclusion about the nature of the Godhead itself—an "eternal truth." Undoubtedly, his own personal life story is a factor, as he himself would be the first to acknowledge.

While I disagree with Jung's conclusion about the metaphysical God (primarily because my experience of the "feeling tone" of that reality is different from his), I want to say that Jung is quite right in raising the philosophical and theological question of the nature of the dualism seemingly present in God. Process theologians are currently exploring this question, along with followers of Tillich and Berdyaev. Tillich posited not evil, but finitude in the Godhead, and, as he said in reply to his critics, "Finitude is not evil, but the potentiality of evil." [10] Few theologians today would question that the negativities of life must in some way be reconciled with, or be encompassed by, the nature of ultimate being. Jung's own myth of God's "need" of humanity (discussed briefly in the next chapter) is moving in the same direction as much current theological thought.

Jung was largely ignored in the theological seminaries until after his death; in most, he still is. Freud was the psychologist who provided a basis for most twentieth-century theologians' understanding of what it means to be human. Jung's failure to engage contemporary theological thought is certainly understandable. They gave him little opportunity to do so during his lifetime. Today the situation is beginning to change. Tillich realized this "error," but mainly after Jung's death, and not long before his own. He is said to have remarked in one of his last seminars at the University of Chicago that if he had enough time left, he would like to move in a "Jungian" direction.

Nevertheless, it is still true that Jung's solution to the problem of evil relies heavily on selected Old Testament imagery and the hermetic philosophy of an earlier day. As a result, the picture of God that he suggested—as unreliable, as now good and now bad, as subject to passing whims—is hardly reconcilable with the view of God presented by the early Christian community (the New Testament). Nor is it consistent with individual personal experiences of a God who is best described as all-encompassing love.

To speak of a "Trinity plus Satan" or a "Trinity plus Mary" (depending upon the polarity with which you are concerned) is a rather crude way of getting at the problem. Furthermore, it is misleading to the average person, for whom Jung was rightly concerned. Neither of those formulations expresses adequately the totality of the very union of opposites which Jung knew to be the psyche's experience. Jung's understanding would be better served by abandoning the symbol of the Trinity altogether.[11]

A possible basis for Jung's deep concern with the symbol of the Trinity is suggested by the story he told in his memoirs about his experience as a boy in a confirmation class his father taught.[12] Jung said that when they got to the passage on the Trinity (to which he had looked forward, since it presented an interesting question—for a change!) his father said that they would skip that section, for he had never understood the Trinity. Jung said he admired his father's honesty at the time, but he was disappointed. In his later years, the son could be said to have offered a kind of justification for the father's problem with the Trinity: it was an appropriate symbol anyway!

In some correspondence with a clergyman, rather late in his life, Jung suggested some pastoral (or therapeutic) reasons why the symbol of the quaternity was to be preferred. He wrote, "With the quaternity the powers of evil, so much greater than man's, are restored to the divine wholeness, whence they originated, even according to Genesis."[13] After all, Jung said, man did not create the serpent. Jung went on to say that if we think of ourselves as the source of evil (while maintaining that all good stems from God), we tend to be filled with satanic pride on the one side and a deep feeling of inferiority on the other. Whereas, he added, if we ascribe the immense power of the opposites to the Deity, we then fall into our modest place as a small image of the Deity. Jung found support for his theory not only in his own psychological experiences and those of his patients, but also in what he called "the historical evidence." By that he referred to the great variety of expressions of four (particularly in mandala configurations) in the history of religion, such as the *Tao*, the four sons of Horus in ancient Egypt, the four evangelists, rose windows, and so on.

Jung was repelled by his early (perhaps literal) understanding of part of the Christian story. The idea of killing, he said, "a human victim to placate the senseless wrath of a God who had created imperfect beings unable to fulfil his expectations poisoned my whole religion."[14] The interpretation to which Jung refers here is a theory from another age by which Christians sought to understand the experience of the "atonement"—that experience of at-one-ment between the good God and the sinful individual, which Jung has taught us to see as a kind of reconciliation of opposites. Psychic reality requires symbolic language for its expression. We can easily share Jung's humane concerns as a young person. If we respond to that story (of the human victim) as Jung did, then we can only say: that symbol is dead for me; it no longer communicates the reality of the experience.

In his myth of the "dark side" of God, Jung suggested another story by which we can seek to come to terms with the reality of existence (which certainly includes the experience of evil). It is a revision of the traditional Christian symbol for the ultimate and infinite. For many, in Jung's experience, it proved to be a story that "worked"—and that is what a "truth" is, he once said. It is not a truth, however, for those whose encounter is with the God of Love, rather than with Jung's God, Abraxas, of whom he speaks in his "Seven Sermons to the Dead." Possibly it is loyalty to that experience, as well as the arguments already considered, that led Jung to make his theory of the "dark side" of God almost a dogma—something not to be questioned.

Jung's challenge to Christianity with his teaching on "the dark side of God" at least says that preaching that holds out "sweet Jesus, meek and mild" is inadequate. The Church in the modern world has not responded adequately to the intellectual questions raised by the presence of evil. In his later writings, Jung is crying out with Job, as well as seeking to "answer" him. He wants a story, a myth of meaning. After a lifetime of working with patients hungry for the answers to the mystery of life and embattled in their own struggle with evil, his own soul was not only angry but in *mourning*. Even earlier, at the midpoint in his own life, Jung's private "visions" (the "Seven Sermons to the Dead" material) portray much "weeping in Jerusalem." The material from the unconscious that he recorded in his private diary is a *lament*, in the classic mythic style. The challenge to the Christian community is to pay attention to those tears—tears in which so many people have found comfort and relief. Jung's followers know that they are not *alone* in being puzzled at the mystery of evil; Jung faced it too. Not only had Jung wrestled with the problem, but he offered them the "grace" of *understanding*. (Jung added a fourth "grace," as he called it, to St. Paul's "faith, hope, and love.")[15]

Jung raised serious questions, and they deserve serious responses. I suggest that a closer look at the symbols and implications of the Christian story reveals more serious and saving answers than many Jungians realize.

Chapter Fifteen

EVIL AND THE RESURRECTION SYMBOL

Charting the relation between Jung's answer to the problem of evil and the Christian response to evil requires a closer look at some symbols in the basic Christian story. Sometimes Jung's ideas can be reconciled with Christianity; in other areas, they cannot. The old story (myth) of a "war in heaven" is one way in which the reality of evil (apart from human choice, but not essentially a part of the Creator) has been portrayed. The symbol of Resurrection was given some attention by Jung, as noted below, but for him it was never significant in the way it is for Christians, namely, as a symbol of the *victory over evil*.

One of Jung's main "myths of meaning" was that God *needs* us—specifically, needs human consciousness. From Jung's psychological perspective, this "need" is for human consciousness; consciousness is what we have to contribute to the world process. Psychology tends to translate human experience into "need" language.

Some resonance with Jung's myth of God's need for us is found in the Judeo-Christian tradition, though theology, beginning with God instead of humanity, tends to speak of the purpose or meaning of God's creation. The Jewish philosopher Martin Buber spoke of God as being "shaped" by human action.[1] William James wondered whether the faithfulness of individuals to their own "over-beliefs" might not "help God," as he said, "to be more effectively faithful to his own greater tasks."[2] Paul Tillich spoke of God's act

of creation as being eternally "driven by a love which finds fulfillment only through the other one who has the freedom to reject
and to accept love." [3] In process theology, God is (to use the phrase
from Charles Wesley's hymn) "pure unbounded love" that *lures* us
into becoming loving and so enhancing the very action of love
itself. [4] In all these approaches, some purpose or meaning is given
to human experience.

Love requires that it be freely offered. Freedom requires consciousness, an awareness of the possibilities of choice. Consciousness *is* involved in the problem of evil; Jung is on the right track.
The question is: Does he foreclose the issue too soon? Does the
fact of the necessity of the possibility of choice (for there to be
love) require that the Creator of that possibility, God, *be* both
good and evil? Or, would it not be more likely (if we assume
meaning and purpose in the world, which Jung does) that we are
presented with choice in order that we may join in the creation of
life's basic reality—love?

In Christian thought, the "need" is related to the fact of *love*.
"God is love" was the experience of the New Testament writers
(I John 4:8). God's purpose for us, as discerned by the early
Christian community, was that we should freely respond with
love—to become loving, as the Creator is. Love longs for love,
and by its action creates love. This action of love is absolutely
fundamental to an understanding of the Christian attitude toward
evil. The action of love can also be translated into the terms of
psychology as the healing unity achieved in an integrated personality.

The discernment of the *unity* of God the Creator and God the
Redeemer was the exciting new truth in the early Christian community. It was the "good news" that (in psychological terms) the
ego's burden did not have to be borne alone. There was an "ad-
vocate," as Job had hoped. The Christ experience was the answer
to Job. In Jung's psychological language, the ego had discovered
the reality of the self. Going beyond Jung's formulation, though

not beyond his experience, as indicated below, the ego discovered that it was *love* that was both the healing and the enabling factor. Love is an *act* in human experience. It requires a story to describe it—it is not a thing you can put under the microscope. Evil is an act also—a rebellion against love.

As far as I can tell from my reading, Jung did not experience a God who loves and forgives, though he clearly knew love as a healing factor in psychotherapy. It is true probably that all our formulations about reality ultimately stem from our own experience of reality. (Jung knew this in his work in psychotherapy—for example, that "only the wounded can heal," that only that which the doctor has put right in himself can he hope to help the patient with.) The contemporary theologian Langdon Gilkey has suggested, for example, that the reason Tillich chose ontological categories to describe God (such as the symbol "ground of being") was that Tillich's *own* experience led him to do so.[5] Tillich's experience was basically that of ontological renewal, of alienation overcome by "new being"—rather than the experience of having guilt removed by a more personal God who loves and forgives.

If love is the fundamental Christian experience, as we have said, then love is, for the Christian, an attribute of ultimate reality, if not ultimate reality itself. "We love because He first loved us." (I John 4:19) Love is the creating, healing factor throughout God's creation, individually and socially. (Some are confident that this can even be observed with respect to their house plants!) Love is an expression of ultimate acceptance. In love the polarities of life are overcome. Experiencing acceptance by another and learning to accept ourselves is also what most of psychotherapy is about.

Love is a mystery. Jung spoke of his encounter with the complexity of this phenomenon. In the section called "Late Thoughts," near the end of his memoirs he wrote:

> I sometimes feel that Paul's words—"Though I speak with the tongues of men and of angels, and have not love"—might

well be the first condition of all cognition and the quintessence of divinity itself. Whatever the learned interpretation may
be of the sentence "God is love," the words affirm the *com-
plexio oppositorum* of the Godhead. In my medical experience
as well as in my own life I have again and again been faced
with the mystery of love, and have never been able to explain
what it is.[6]

Love is a mystery not to be comprehended by us, Jung said, and
he went on to list some of the opposites that are encompassed by
love. We go beyond our ability when we try to say in just what
the paradox consists, he said. It is evidently something of this
complexity that made Jung want to include the opposites of good
and evil in the Godhead—to include the Devil.

Undoubtedly many Christians have not given the devil his due.
The optimistic "liberal" theology of the early twentieth century
generally had little to say about "the world, the flesh, and the
devil." Sin was more *error* than something that "dwells in me," as
St. Paul had felt. However, Christianity has never gone so far as
to deny the reality of evil (as some religious philosophies have
done).

The problem of evil is central to Christianity. The pervasive
fact of evil seems to contradict the Christian affirmation that ultimate reality is love. On the other hand, it is the victory over evil
that was the essential proclamation of the early Christian community. At first blush, the Christian position seems to be (in the
face of evil) a great stoic cry of "Nevertheless!" It *is* that in part,
but it is also much more. The Christian experience of "God's love
poured into our hearts" is an experience of *gift*—a gift with power,
which is the meaning of the theological term *grace*. In fact, the
central symbol of the Christian faith (the Cross) points to the reality of evil. However, that same symbol also points to the power
of love to conquer evil—the Resurrection.

It is this last point that I find missing in Jung's theologizing.
Jung hopes that when human consciousness is raised, the "good"

will be chosen. His symbolic expression for that force which seeks to overcome evil is largely missing. I think it is fair to say that his system uses "borrowed capital" that has been stored up by the Judeo-Christian tradition. The assumption that "the good" is real (is a possible choice) and that it "works" (is therefore "true") still lingers on, even in our post-Christian world.

If Jung meant for us to take seriously his discussion of the "three plus four," then he offers us a symbol in which God is at least three-fourths good. For the average person, I doubt that this symbol will penetrate the depths and "make present" the uniting reality. In the Apollinarian controversy of the fourth century, the Church found, in its attempt to express its experience of Jesus as the Christ, that the formulation that made him "two-thirds human and one-third divine" was inadequate as a symbol for the *power* of reuniting love that had been experienced by many as an unexpected gift.

Along with the alchemists, Jung tended to make the individual the Redeemer, rather than God's Christ. It is, to that extent, "work" (something earned) rather than a "free gift." It is no longer the "good news" that so excited the many slaves in the early Christian community. Yet Jung also knew the element of "gift" in his experience as a psychotherapist, though he tells us that he had to say "the psyche has awakened to spontaneous activity," thus avoiding any reference to God with most of his patients (because it reminded them too much of what they had to reject in the first place.)[7] Jung knew the experience of *grace* (a gift with power) in his psychotherapeutic work, but in the theories with which he attempted to "answer Job" he did not include that datum of experience.

For the Christian, evil is historical—it is something that comes into the world after creation, as the old story says. "Redemption" is therefore possible. The Christian position is not one of passively accepting evil as a necessary fact of existence; rather, evil is something to do battle with, as Luther's hymn so vividly suggests ("Though this world with devils filled . . .").

The late Esther Harding, one of the founders of the Analytical Psychology Club in New York, wrote, "But if God is the summum bonum, a formulation that excludes evil in its transcendent aspect, then all evil must originate in man himself." [8] Harding's statement ignores what the old stories of the Creation and of the Fall have to say. In speculating on the mystery, Christian thought concluded that the good God's creation included more than just humans among the creatures with free will. There were "good" angels, but also "fallen" angels. That is to say, the power of choice may extend beyond the state of consciousness that we know. The autonomous forces of the unconscious that Jung explored are also part of God's creation. ("Maker . . . of all that is, seen and unseen," the Nicene Creed affirms.) The story of a war in heaven, and of a rebellion of some spirits, expresses this psychic reality—that there is good and evil at work outside the acts of human consciousness. Thomas Aquinas's description of an angel as a "thought that thinks itself" is quite in accord with Jung's description of autonomous psychic complexes. [9] In commenting on this "invisible" realm, Tillich spoke of psychology's "rediscovery" of angels as archetypes of the collective unconscious. In his *Systematic Theology* he wrote, "In our terminology we could say that the angels are concrete-poetic symbols of the structures or powers of being." [10] It is interesting to compare this with Jung's supposition that the archetypes are products of the long evolutionary development of life on our planet. At any rate, perhaps Jung's challenge will provide contemporary theology with a new incentive to take cognizance once again of the reality of evil and its power, over and beyond human choosing, as Jung felt it should.

Because the theory did not seem to take seriously the presence of evil in the world, Jung always objected to Augustine's *privatio boni* doctrine (that evil is the *absence* of good). To Jung, such an idea did not do justice to our encounter with evil, both in ourselves (a will other than that of the ego), and in the world at large (Auschwitz, for example). In wrestling with Jung's idea about the nature of ultimate being (whether "good" or only three-fourths "good"), I was interested to observe the arguments made by the cult of Satan worship that developed in the late 1960s. In defending the value of Satan worship, its proponents presented it as the "opposite" of Christianity, which, it was said, meant "turning Christianity on its head." Doing all the things Christianity forbids is "healthy" for the body and for the personality, it was argued. Yet in making the case for evil, the proponents could find no way to commend these activities, except to present them as something "good"! Is "good" what the "real" always is?

The theory of Christian experience, that there is a power for good (that accepts us despite whatever—just as we are) that is able to overcome the evil, is completed when that power for good is made manifest in the victory of the man Jesus over the "last enemy," death. The "Resurrection experiences" (however understood, as discussed below) became the symbol of this victory. The reconciliation experience (the at-one-ment experience) was proclaimed as *Christus Victor*.[11] The evil forces were conquered. The rebellion was defeated. "Nothing can separate us from the love of God," St. Paul wrote to the Christians in Rome, "neither death, nor life, nor angels, nor principalities, nor height, nor depth, nor anything else in all creation." (Romans 8:38–39) The Resurrection experiences, which the early Christians frequently have such a difficult time expressing concretely, comprise the part of the "Christ experience" that speaks most specifically to the problem of evil. Furthermore, the Resurrection is a symbol expressing *joy*. That is what all the "shouting" and glorious Easter music is about. The power of love is triumphant.

Jung, by his own admission, wrote very little on the symbol of the Resurrection, despite his great attention to the Mass, the Trinity, and to so many of the other symbols of the Christian faith. In the recently published volume 18 of his collected works, there is a five-page comment, "On Resurrection," written by Jung in response to an inquiry as to whether he had written anything on the Resurrection. In this short essay, Jung points out the difference between the Resurrection as historical fact (doubtful, he concludes) and Resurrection as a psychological event (an inevitable concomitant of the archetype of the self). From his lifetime of study Jung concluded that the psyche was not bounded by space and time, which in turn, suggested the possibility of some kind of psychical existence, or "life after death." He viewed the Christian symbol of the Resurrection as a response to the need for a materialistic expression of psychic reality. All primitives, including the primitive Christians, he said, need a concrete, materialistic event that can be seen by the eyes and touched by the hands. He added, "Even in modern times people cannot easily grasp the reality of a psychic event, unless it is concrete at the same time."[12] (For Jung, of course, we must always remember that a psychic reality is just as "real" as a physical reality.)

Jung is quite right about one function of the symbol of the Resurrection—namely, that it points to some form of a life after death. However, it has even more fundamental meanings. In his essay "Concerning Rebirth," Jung mentions Resurrection as one of the "forms of rebirth."[13] The idea of rebirth and transformation is, of course, of the utmost importance to his understanding of psychic development. It is also basic to the Christian symbol system. For the Christian, rebirth is made possible through God's power and love. The idea of *gift* is fundamental to the understanding of the symbol Resurrection. It is an experience of the power of love that makes possible being "born again." It is a gift of the Spirit (John 3:3–8). The *present* experience of having God's love "poured into our hearts" (Romans 5:5) is what provides the basis for a *hope* of a life in "the world to come." "Born again" Christians have already experienced rebirth; it does not depend upon some future existence (although the hope for that is not precluded).

Resurrection and the Easter liturgy symbolize for the Christian the possibility of a new life, both *now* and eternally. It is not a symbol that denies the experience of evil, but, on the contrary, emphasizes its destructiveness. It asserts a victory over the autonomous forces of evil present in the world. Christians have never said that all the forces encountered in the unconscious are "good," any more than Jung did. That is why St. Paul spoke of one of the gifts of God's Holy Spirit as that of the "discernment of spirits." On this point, Jung, too, once commented that the "discernment of spirits" was no simple matter. That was why, he said, the Church reserved the right to act as a director of conscience.[14]

The New Testament accounts of the Resurrection are (as Jung said about the dogma of the bodily assumption of Mary) a slap in the face of rationality. For many in the modern world, this has been the "stumbling block" in accepting the credibility of Christianity, as it was in New Testament times. Even for some today who think of themselves as Christians the story of the empty tomb seems doubtful as historical fact in the modern, materialistic sense, but, with Jung, they find that the story expressed and continues to express the reality of a psychic event. The *fact* that a number of people had such an experience, sometimes seeing the risen Jesus, sometimes only hearing his voice (even if understood as a psychic experience) *is* a historical fact. The Church, which originated in this community of people who had the experience, is a historical fact. The Resurrection is an essential part, not only of the faith of Christians, but of their experience down through the centuries.

The Cross and the Resurrection are symbols of the Christian answer to the problem of evil. As living symbols, they are grounded in personal experience. It is unfortunate that Jung did not examine them more fully. Additional psychological interpretation of these symbols is needed in relation to the shadow and the vast human experience of evil. Such an investigation would be far more fruitful than further pursuit of Jung's theory of evil in the Godhead—certainly for Christians, and quite possibly for others as well.

Chapter Sixteen

THE HOLY SPIRIT
AND THE NEW AGE

The answer to Jung's challenge, for the Christian community, may well be to give fresh consideration to the doctrine of the Holy Spirit. The Holy Spirit is the symbol by which Christians (and Jews as well) have expressed the personal experience of God by the individual. Such experiences must be listened to and interpreted. From a deeper understanding of our relationship to the Holy Spirit, a new age of consciousness may rise.

Jung himself thought that Christianity's answer to his challenge lay in this direction. He found encouragement for this idea in the fact that William Temple, then Archbishop of Canterbury, once remarked to him that "the Church has not done everything it might have been expected to do in regard to the doctrine of the Holy Ghost."[1] That further development needed consists of providing the symbolic (doctrinal and liturgical) vessels for interpreting and incorporating individual experiences of God. Jung insisted, as we have seen, that the rebirth and transformative experiences represented in the dogma and liturgy of the Christian community must become a matter of individual psychic experience.

As already noted, Jung held that Christianity had earlier rendered a service by helping individuals to get control over their instincts. Now, Jung felt, with the age of divided consciousness (the age of Pisces) almost over, a further service is needed. He sometimes spoke of this as the need for a further development of the Christian myth. It is not that Christianity is finished, he said, but rather that our conception and interpretation of it have become antiquated in the face of the present world situation. He wrote, "The Christian symbol is a living thing that carries in itself the seeds of further development."[2] It remains for us, he said, to meditate again, and more thoroughly, on the Christian premises.

In Jung's view, our religious symbols are a response to our developing consciousness. Thanks to questioning minds, such as the author of Job, human consciousness led us to recognize the opposites contained in our image of God. This led, in turn, to the breaking apart of these opposites, and to our choosing the good for our model. For us, God incarnated himself in the good, Jung said. The split into Christ and Anti-Christ was helpful for us in our development of consciousness; the differentiation of opposites was a necessary concomitant of consciousness. It was a tremendous educative task that Christianity performed for the ancient world. Moreover, Jung suggested, further service could still be rendered by the Church if it were to provide the symbol system for aiding us in our journey toward a new age—an age in which the wholeness of the psyche would be experienced.

This "Christian era" has even, synchronistically, been expressed in astrological lore as the age of Pisces—two fishes swimming in different directions, thus representing the split. In his book *Aion*, Jung speculated that the new age might well be one in which the opposites are overcome, but not with a return to an unconscious whole. Rather, in the new age, that which had been unconscious would be integrated into consciousness. As Jung saw it, the Christian myth needed reinterpretation, a further development of the idea of the Holy Spirit. This "third stage" Jung describes in his essay on the Trinity.[3] We need to incarnate the union of opposites formerly projected on the "unconscious" Yahweh, but now with the benefit of consciousness. Jung spoke of it as the continuing Incarnation. He also referred to this development as the "Christification of many." This reinterpretation of the Christian myth, if accomplished, could heal the projected split in the world, that is, the alienation expressed in the political world, in the ecology question, and so on.

The task to which we are summoned, in Jung's view, is one of finding a means of uniting the opposites in ourselves. That is the symbolic meaning of each person taking up the Cross of Christ— to experience that reconciliation of the opposites within him- or herself. Obviously God does not want us to remain as children, waiting for a parent to do the job for us.

In some correspondence in the 1950s with a Christian clergyman, Jung pointed out that while we are inspired by the Holy Spirit for a particular task (i.e., to bring to consciousness the problem of the union of opposites), we are still in danger of succumbing to "inflation." We are liable to identify the divine Spirit with our own minds, and to feel that we have a Messianic mission—even leading us to force tyrannous doctrines upon each other. Such an inflation is well known in human experience and history. To avoid that danger, we need to disidentify our minds from the small voice within. One must listen to the inner voice attentively, intelligently—and also critically, for Jung said that the voice one hears has two aspects.[4] It is, itself, a union of opposites. One has the task of choice, of discernment.

Jung emphasized our responsibility. We must choose, and not just follow every leading of the unconscious; the burden of choice is ours. That is what follows from the achievement of consciousness. Jung's "doctrine of man," his view of consciousness, is a restatement of a very basic biblical theme to be found in both the New Testament and the Hebrew scriptures—namely, human responsibility before God.

In the same late correspondence, Jung said that while his comments might appear as a sort of theological speculation, they were, in fact, based upon his experience in the treatment of neuroses in our day. They were the modern person's perplexities expressed in symbolic terms. You could also express it in psychological language, Jung said.

For instance, instead of using the term God you say "unconscious," instead of Christ "self," instead of incarnation "integration of the unconscious," instead of salvation or redemption "individuation," instead of crucifixion or sacrifice on the Cross "realization of the four functions" or of "wholeness."[5]

Jung did not intend to belittle religious tradition by noting how far it coincided with psychological experience. On the contrary, he said, such comparisons should provide a welcome aid in understanding religious traditions. He wrote:

Today Christianity is devitalized by its remoteness from the spirit of the times. It stands in need of a new union with, or relation to, the atomic age, which is a unique novelty in history. . . . It is my practical experience that psychological understanding immediately revivifies the essential Christian ideas and fills them with the breath of life. This is because our worldly light, i.e., scientific knowledge and understanding, coincides with the symbolic statement of the myth, whereas previously we were unable to bridge the gulf between knowing and believing.[6]

As noted in the last chapter, I cannot accept Jung's conclusion about the place of evil in the Godhead, though I have no problem with his emphasis on the reality of evil as a *force* in the world. Jung's emotional opposition to the *privatio boni* theory (evil defined as the "absence of good") was probably based on his private experience of unconscious forces. My own experience (and that of others as well) has been that ultimate reality has the character of *love*, which to me is good, although it certainly increases one's openness to pain and suffering. As Jung himself stated, one cannot argue with experience. Perhaps we have to wait here for a *consensus gentium* (as Jung would say), that is, a general agreement by those who "have ears to hear." "Discernment of spirits" is not an easy matter, as Jung himself said once. Archbishop William

Temple said that "private revelations" are not to be trusted by themselves—we have to test them against our knowledge of the "true Mediator," that is, the Christ experience of the Church.[7] We have to see what the Christian community concludes over the centuries. Jung might express a similar idea in this way: we have to see what an observation of the archetypes of the collective unconscious reveals.

Happily, and as one might expect, this psychological recognition of the way the Holy Spirit operates on us is both Catholic and Protestant; both branches of Christendom may feel vindicated. The emphasis on private personal experience that Jung insisted upon is the truth to which Protestantism has continued to witness. Dogma alone is not enough, unless it is personally experienced. On the other hand, Jung's notion that ultimate truth continues to be expressed by the archetypes of the collective unconscious is embodied in the Catholic teaching on the authority of *tradition* (as well as scripture). Jung's prime example was, as we have seen, the response of the Pope to the psychic need for a symbolic representation of the feminine in heaven. Jung said that ultimately the archetype of wholeness would express itself; God would be heard.

Any development in Christianity's understanding of the Holy Spirit will take time and the careful work of many, who, seeking to carry out the theologians' task, will attempt to translate the truths of individual experience into the thought forms of our day. Jung has suggested some possibilities by viewing the age of the Holy Spirit as one in which the dialogue between the unconscious and consciousness reaches a new level. For example, in the Western version of the Church's Nicene Creed, the Holy Spirit is said to "proceed from the Father, *and the Son.*" In Jung's language, this could be understood to mean that the experience of the Holy Spirit is the result of a coming together of both the unconscious (the Father-Creator) and the state of consciousness (to which the Christian era witnessed). Jesus told his disciples, "It is to your advantage that I go away, for if I do not go away, the Counselor will not come to you; but if I go, I will send him to you." (John 16:7) That is to say, in Jung's psychological language, it is necessary that the projections be withdrawn from the human Jesus and from the evil with which he contended. We must grow until we attain "the measure of the fullness of Christ" (Ephesians 4:13). We must exercise choice and become creators of the good, as God has called us to be. The presence of the Holy Spirit means that we have the benefit of help from beyond our own conscious willing and striving. We can become the dwelling place of God (if we avoid the inflation about which Jung warned). We are in a new state of communion with God. St. Paul spoke of his experience as that of "the Christ within."

In whatever way the new age is understood or symbolically appropriated by an individual, it will be mediated by a community, which provides us with the tools for interpretation (as discussed in chapter 13). By further attention to understanding what is meant by the *Holy Spirit*, the community of the Church has the opportunity to lead us into a new relationship with God. The experience has always been real for some; but further teaching on the Holy Spirit may open that door to experience for others. That is what Jung hoped for.

A new appreciation of the Holy Spirit may also provide a doorway for a reunion of Catholicism and Protestantism—perhaps even Judaism, whose scriptures also are not without many references to God's holy spirit. A favorite passage of the pentecostal movement has been:

> And it shall come to pass afterward,
>   that I will pour out my spirit on all flesh;
> your sons and your daughters shall prophesy,
>   and old men shall dream dreams,
>   and your young men shall see visions.
> Even upon the menservants and maidservants
>   in those days, I will pour out my spirit. (Joel 1:28–29)

In the Hasidic tradition of Judaism, a *zaddik* is a "teacher" who not only "has knowledge" of God's laws, but who is possessed by God's holy spirit.

Jung postulated a theory that he called *synchronicity*, speaking of it as "an acausal connecting principle."[8] The data supporting this hypothesis are all those occasions when there seems to be a coming together of events in time with a common or related meaning—yet with no causal connection. In this concept of synchronicity Jung found some evidence for postulating a meaning present in the universe over and beyond human consciousness. There was only one reality—psychic and physical simply being two sides of the same coin—and in this one reality, *orderedness* expresses itself. Jung said that we know as little of a supreme being as we do of matter. "But," he added, "there is as little doubt of the existence of a supreme being as of matter. The world beyond is a reality, an experiential fact."[9] The problem is that we simply do not understand it.

The story of humanity is, as Jung pointed out to us, a story of developing consciousness; our movement is toward consciousness. As we have seen, Jung, in his later writing, often spoke about our movement today into an Aquarian Age. The age of the split consciousness symbolized by Pisces is passing. The astrological symbol for the new age has a human figure carrying a pail of water. Water is a well-attested symbol of the unconscious. What would this mean symbolically? Is there a new relationship with the unconscious in store for us?

Jung suggested that the end of the story has not been reached. Life entails choice. There is both dark and light. The "Fall" into consciousness (as Jung interpreted the old story of a Garden of Eden) was a tremendous leap forward in the story of life on our planet. Is there another leap ahead? Perhaps the story of human development will lead beyond the split. The last book of the New Testament (whose images so fascinated Jung, as he indicates in his book *Answer to Job*) recounts an ancient vision of a "new Jerusalem," a new heaven and a new earth. It undoubtedly expresses a human longing. While it is in no way a proof of such a possibility, Jung has taught us not to disregard what is at least a fact of the psyche. The John on the isle of Patmos who had a terrible vision of the presence of evil in his world also had the vision of "a new heaven and a new earth." The story did not end for him with the acknowledgement of evil as a fact of life. It moved beyond the tension of opposites. Looking through a glass darkly, as St. Paul said, is not so easy, but perhaps we can hope that the myth of the new Jerusalem will one day be seen as a symbolic foretaste of that which is to come in the continuing unfolding of our story.

Our participation in the cosmic process calls for us to continue in our development toward becoming aware of the whole. Jung expressed this in his myth of God's need of us, which he found expressed in the Western mystics, as well as in his own experience, forming the basis for his own personal myth of meaning. As he wrote in a letter once, "We are still looking back to the pentecostal events in a dazed way instead of looking forward to the goal the Spirit is leading us to." [10]

That was his vision, his hope. The future of Christianity, as he saw it, lies in the realization of the Christ within each person. That is surely the meaning of the Holy Spirit understood as present in each person. The Christ experience is, in his psychological language, the encounter with the self. It is not a matter of making out of each person a "God," but on the contrary, realizing that within each person lies the potentiality of responding to God by bringing that encounter into consciousness. This is our task. The challenge for Christianity lies in its opportunity to provide us with the framework of symbolic meaning within which we can carry out our task. It was Jung's (almost despairing) hope that the Christian community would take up this challenge.

NOTES

Chapter 1. The Pastor of Souls

1 See Jung's comment along this line in his correspondence with H. L. Philp in *The Collected Works of C. G. Jung*, ed. Sir Herbert Read, et. al., trans. R. F. C. Hull (2d ed. rev., Bollingen Series XX; Princeton, N.J.: Princeton University Press, 1970), XVIII, p. 707.

2 Jung, *Collected Works*, XI, p. 469.

3 Jung, *Collected Works*, XIII, p. 50.

4 *Ibid.*

5 *Ibid.*, pp. 50–51.

6 Jung, *Collected Works*, XIV, p. 551.

7 *Ibid.*, p. 553.

8 Paul Tillich, *The Courage to Be* (New Haven: Yale University Press, 1952), p. 47.

9 Jung, *Collected Works*, VIII, p. 356.

10 C. G. Jung, *Modern Man in Search of a Soul*, trans. W. S. Dell and Cary F. Baynes (New York: Harcourt, Brace & World, 1933), p. 225.

11 Jung, *Collected Works*, XI, p. 469.

12 *Ibid.*, p. 331.

13 *Ibid.*, p. 332.

14 *Ibid.*, p. 337.

15 *Ibid.*, p. 334.

Chapter 2. Psychic Reality and Psychic Energy

1 Jung, *Collected Works*, VIII, p. 354.

2 Jung, *Collected Works*, XIII, p. 42.

3 *Ibid.*

4 Jung, *Collected Works*, VIII, p. 326.

5 C. G. Jung and W. Pauli, *The Interpretation of Nature and the Psyche* (Bollingen Series LI; New York: Pantheon Books, 1955), p. 208.

[6] Jung, *Collected Works*, XIV, p. 538.

[7] *Ibid.*

[8] Paul Tillich, "The Relation of Religion and Health: Historical Considerations and Theoretical Questions," *The Review of Religion*, May (New York: Columbia University Press, 1946), pp. 380, 382.

[9] Jung, *Collected Works*, XVII, p. 86.

[10] Jung, *Collected Works*, XVIII, p. 33.

[11] *Ibid.* Similarly, in his essay "On Psychic Energy," Jung suggested that one's view of physical events from either a mechanistic or an energic standpoint depended primarily on one's psychological attitude. See: Jung, *Collected Works*, VIII, pp. 3–5.

[12] Jung, *Collected Works*, IV, p. 255.

[13] Jolande Jacobi, *The Psychology of C. G. Jung*, trans. Ralph Manheim (6th ed. rev.; London: Routledge and Kegan Paul, 1962), p. 1.

[14] Jung, *Collected Works*, XI, p. 359.

[15] Jung, *Collected Works*, XVI, p. 153. See also Jung's essay "The Concept of the Libido," in Jung, *Collected Works*, V, pp. 132–41.

[16] See Jung's illustrations of this in his section on "The Transformation of Libido," in Jung, *Collected Works*, V, pp. 142–170.

[17] Jung, *Collected Works*, VIII, p. 45.

[18] *Ibid.*, p. 27.

[19] Jacobi, *op. cit.*, p. 59.

[20] Jung, *Collected Works*, VII, p. 110.

Chapter 3. The Structure of the Psyche

[1] Jung, *Collected Works*, XVIII, p. 7.

[2] Jung, *Modern Man*, p. 85.

[3] Jung, *Collected Works*, XVIII, p. 15.

[4] Jung, *Collected Works*, X, p. 471.

[5] Jung, *Collected Works*, VI, p. 489.

[6] Jung, *Collected Works*, IX (I), p. 123.

[7] Jung, *Collected Works*, VIII, p. 158.

[8] *Ibid.*

[9] Jung, *Collected Works*, XVIII, p. 42. Jung discussed this same case elsewhere in his writings: Jung, *Collected Works*, V, pp. 101–102; IX (I), pp. 50–53; and VIII, pp. 111, 150–151.

[10] S. Freud, *The Ego and the Id*, trans. Joan Riviere, rev. and newly ed. by James Strachey (New York: W. W. Norton & Company, 1960), p. 28.

¹¹Jung, *Collected Works*, XVIII, p. 73.

¹²*Ibid.*, p. 11.

¹³Edward F. Edinger, M.D., "An Outline of Analytical Psychology," *Quadrant*, I, (Spring, 1968), p. 11.

¹⁴Jung, *Collected Works*, IX (I), p. 60.

¹⁵Jacobi, *op. cit.*, p. 111.

¹⁶On the *self*, see Jung's *Aion*, the subtitle of which is "Researches into the Phenomenology of the Self," *Collected Works*, IX (II), pp. 22–35.

¹⁷Jung, *Collected Works*, VII, p. 219.

¹⁸*Ibid.*, p. 236.

¹⁹*Ibid.*, p. 238.

²⁰Jung, *Collected Works*, X, p. 463.

Chapter 4. The Stages of Life

¹See Jung's essay, "The Stages of Life," *Collected Works*, VIII, pp. 387–403.

²Jung, *Collected Works*, XVII, p. 119.

³*Ibid.*, p. 52.

⁴Michael Fordham, "On the Origins of the Ego in Childhood," *Studien Zur Analytischen Psychologie C. G. Jungs*, ed. Das Curatorium des C. G. Jung-Institutes, Zurich (Zurich: Rascher Verlag, 1955), pp. 80–105.

⁵Paul Ricoeur, "Symbol: Food for Thought," *Philosophy Today*, IV, (Spring, 1960), pp. 196–207. Compare Paul Tillich's attempt to allow for a place in history (for the experience of existence) when one returns to "essence" by the process of "essentialization." See Paul Tillich, *Systematic Theology* (3d ed. rev., Chicago: University of Chicago Press, 1963), III, pp. 406–423.

⁶C. G. Jung, *Memories, Dreams, Reflections*, ed. Aniela Jaffe, trans. Richard and Clara Winston (New York: Random House, 1963), p. 348.

⁷Jung, *Collected Works*, XVI, p. 39.

⁸Jung, *Collected Works*, VII, p. 46.

⁹Jung, *Collected Works*, IX (I), p. 11.

¹⁰Jung, *Collected Works*, XIV, p. 555.

¹¹Jung, *Collected Works*, V, p. xxiv.

¹²Jung, *Collected Works*, XI, p. 468.

Chapter 5. The Process of Psychotherapy

¹Jung, *Collected Works*, VII, p. 46.

²Jung, *Memories, Dreams, Reflections*, p. 150.

[3] Jung, *Collected Works*, XVI, p. 327.

[4] Jung, *Collected Works*, VII, p. 45.

[5] Jung, *Collected Works*, XVIII, p. 493.

[6] Jung, *Collected Works*, XVI, p. 116.

[7] Jung, *Collected Works*, IV, p. 278.

[8] Jung, *Collected Works*, XI, p. 596.

[9] Jung, *Memories, Dreams, Reflections*, p. 134.

[10] Quoted by Jolande Jacobi in *Psychological Reflections: An Anthology of the Writings of C. G. Jung*; Harper Torchbooks, The Bollingen Library, (New York: Harper & Row, 1961), p. 284.

[11] Jung, *Collected Works*, XVIII, p. 110.

[12] *Ibid.*, p. 102.

[13] *Ibid.*, pp. 86–87.

[14] Jung, *Collected Works*, XVI, pp. 163–323.

[15] Jung, *Collected Works*, VIII, p. 68.

[16] Jung, *Collected Works*, XVIII, p. 172. See also Jung's discussion of active imagination in: Jung, *Collected Works*, VII, "The Relations between the Ego and the Unconscious," pp. 222–223; VIII, "The Transcendent Function," pp. 81–82; IX (I), "The Concept of the Collective Unconscious," p. 49; IX (I), "The Psychological Aspects of the Kore," p. 190; XI, "Psychological Commentary on the Tibetan Book of the Great Liberation," p. 496; XII, *Psychology and Alchemy*, p. 255; and XIV, *Mysterium Coniunctionis*, pp. 494–496.

[17] Jung, *Collected Works*, X, p. 280.

[18] Jung, *Collected Works*, IX (I), p. 68.

Chapter 6. Individuation and the Problem of Opposites

[1] Jung, *Collected Works*, XIV, p. 249.

[2] Jung, *Collected Works*, XIII, p. 6.

[3] *Ibid.*, p. 245.

[4] Jung, *Collected Works*, XI, p. 17.

[5] *Ibid.*, p. 291.

[6] *Ibid.*, p. 292.

[7] Jung, *Collected Works*, XIV, p. 334.

[8] Jung, *Collected Works*, VIII, p. 354.

[9] Jung, *Collected Works*, XIV, p. 346.

[10] *Ibid.*, p. 253.

[11] Jung, *Collected Works*, XI, p. 77.

[12] *Ibid.*, p. 79.

[13] *Ibid.*, p. 83.

Chapter 7. *The Uniting Quality of Symbols*

[1] C. G. Jung, *Man and His Symbols* (New York: Dell Publishing Co., 1964), p. 4.

[2] Freud, *The Ego and the Id*, p. 11.

[3] Jung, *Collected Works*, VI, p. 63n.

[4] Gordon W. Allport, *The Person in Psychology* (Boston: Beacon Press, 1968), p. 21.

[5] Jung, *Collected Works*, V, p. 77.

[6] Jung, *Collected Works*, VI, pp. 473–474.

[7] See Paul Tillich's discussion of the distinction between signs and symbols in *Dynamics of Faith;* Harper Colophon Books (New York: Harper & Row, 1957), pp. 41–43.

[8] Jung, *Collected Works*, VI, p. 477.

[9] Jung, *Man and His Symbols*, p. 42.

[10] *Ibid.*, p. 78.

[11] *Ibid.*

[12] *Ibid.*, p. 84.

[13] *Ibid.*

[14] William James, *The Varieties of Religious Experience;* The Modern Library (New York: Random House, 1902), p. 8.

[15] S. Freud, *The Future of an Illusion*, trans. W. D. Robson-Scott, rev. and newly ed. by James Strachey; Anchor Books (Garden City, NY: Doubleday & Company, 1964), p. 89.

[16] C. G. Jung, *Letters*, ed. Gerhard Adler, in collaboration with Aniela Jaffe, trans. R. F. C. Hull, Vol. II, Bollingen Series XCV:II (Princeton, N.J.: Princeton University Press, 1975), p. 7.

[17] See Jung's essay "The Transcendent Function," *Collected Works*, VIII, pp. 69–91.

Chapter 8. *Myth as Meaning-Giver*

[1] Jung, *Collected Works*, IX (I), p. 180.

[2] Jung, *Collected Works*, XIII, pp. 11–12. Jung said that this distant psychic heritage also accounted for the psychological parallelisms with animals. Perhaps Jung has here supplied some support for the human-animal analogy so popular in behavioristic psychology.

³Jung, *Collected Works*, XI, pp. 303–304. Jung observed in a footnote that his theory that the psyche was not a *tabula rasa*, but on the contrary, brought with it instinctive conditions, just as the body did, was not compatible with a Marxist philosophy.

⁴Bronislaw Malinowski, *Magic, Science and Religion*; Anchor Books (Garden City, NY: Doubleday & Company, 1954), p. 108.

⁵Jung, *Collected Works*, IX (I), p. 154.

⁶Mircea Eliade, *Myth and Reality*, trans. Willard R. Trask; Harper Torchbooks (New York and Evanston: Harper & Row, 1963), p. 1.

⁷Joseph Campbell, *The Masks of God: Occidental Mythology* (New York: The Viking Press, 1964), pp. 519 ff.

⁸Laurens van der Post, *Patterns of Renewal*, Pendle Hill pamphlet No. 121 (Lebanon, Penn.: printed by Sowers Printing Co., 1962), p. 9.

⁹Frances G. Wickes, *The Inner World of Choice* (New York: Harper & Row, 1963), p. xv.

Chapter 9. Religious Experience as a Union of Opposites

¹William James, *The Varieties of Religious Experience*, p. 27.

²*Ibid.*, p. 53.

³Paul Tillich, *Christianity and the Encounter of the World Religions* (New York: Columbia University Press, 1963), p. 4.

⁴Tillich, *Dynamics of Faith*, pp. 30–35.

⁵Jung, *Collected Works*, XI, p. 7.

⁶Jung, *Collected Works*, XIII, p. 51.

⁷See Tillich's discussion of spirit as a dimension of man in Vol. III of his *Systematic Theology*.

⁸Jung, *Collected Works*, XII, pp. 14, 17.

⁹Jung, *Collected Works*, XI, p. 156.

¹⁰*Ibid.*, p. 341.

¹¹*Ibid.*

¹²*Ibid.*, p. 346.

¹³*Ibid.*, p. 408.

¹⁴Jung, *Collected Works*, XIV, p. 554.

¹⁵Jung, *Collected Works*, XI, p. 295.

¹⁶*Ibid.*

¹⁷*Ibid.*, p. 294.

Chapter 10. The Language of Religion

¹Jung, *Memories, Dreams, Reflections*, p. 325.

²Jung, *Collected Works*, XIV, p. 197.

³ Jung, *Collected Works*, XI, p. 409.
⁴ Dag Hammarskjöld, *Markings*, trans. Leif Sjoberg and W. H. Auden (London: Faber and Faber, 1964), p. 10.
⁵ Jung, *Collected Works*, XI, p. 62.
⁶ Cf. Tillich, *Dynamics of Faith*, pp. 44-45.
⁷ In this discussion of myth and Christianity, I am indebted to John Knox. See his *Myth and Truth* (Charlottesville: The University Press of Virginia, 1964), especially pp. 29 and 44.
⁸ Jung, *Collected Works*, IX (I), p. 105.
⁹ Jung, *Collected Works*, XI, pp. 201-296.
¹⁰ Jung, *Collected Works*, XIV, p. 336, footnote 297.
¹¹ C. G. Jung, *Letters*, Vol. I, p. 348.

Chapter 11. The Problem with Dogma

¹ Jung, Collected Works, IX (II), pp. 174-75.
² Jung, *Collected Works*, XIII, p. 14.
³ *Ibid.*, p. 10.
⁴ Jung, *Collected Works*, IX (II), p. 176.
⁵ *Ibid.*, p. 178.
⁶ *Aion, Answer to Job, Mysterium Coniunctionis*, and *Memories, Dreams, Reflections* all refer to this symbolic event. His introduction to *Man and His Symbols* and his essay on synchronicity do not.
⁷ Jung, *Collected Works*, XI, p. 8.
⁸ Jung, *Collected Works*, XI, p. 48.
⁹ Jung, *Letters*, Vol. I, p. 346.
¹⁰ Jung, *Collected Works*, XI, p. 46.
¹¹ *Ibid.*, p. 200.
¹² Claxton Monro, William S. Taegel, and Witnessing Laymen, *Witnessing Laymen Make Living Churches* (Waco, Texas: Word Books, 1968), pp. 34-39.
¹³ Jung, *Collected Works*, XI, p. 105.
¹⁴ *Ibid.*

Chapter 12. The Voice of God Can Still Be Heard!

¹ Aniela Jaffe, *The Myth of Meaning in the Work of C. G. Jung*, trans. R. F. C. Hull (London: Hodder and Stoughton, 1970), p. 53.
² Jung, *Collected Works*, XII, p. 11, footnote 6.
³ Jung, *Collected Works*, XI, pp. 345-346. See also Edward C. Whit-

mont, *The Symbolic Quest* (Published by G. P. Putnam's Sons, New York, for the C. G. Jung Foundation for Analytical Psychology, 1969), p. 230.

⁴*The Book of Common Prayer* (New York: The Church Pension Fund, 1945), p. 17.

⁵Edward C. Whitmont, "Religious Aspects of Life Problems in Analysis," in Eleanor Bertine, M. Esther Harding, Edward C. Whitmont, *Three Papers on Jung's Approach to Religion*, reprinted from *Spring* 1958 and *Spring* 1959 (New York: The Analytical Psychology Club of New York, 1958, 1959), p. 43.

⁶Jung, *Memories, Dreams, Reflections*, p. 280.

⁷Jung, *Collected Works*, XI, p. 340.

⁸Hammarskjöld, *Markings*, p. 169.

⁹Jung, *Collected Works*, XI, p. 87.

¹⁰*Ibid.*, p. 88.

¹¹*Ibid.*, p. 153.

¹²*Ibid.*

¹³*Ibid.*, pp. 153–154.

¹⁴Jung, *Collected Works*, XIV, p. 124.

¹⁵Jung, *Collected Works*, XI, p. 409.

¹⁶Jung, *Collected Works*, V, p. xxv.

¹⁷Jaffe, *The Myth of Meaning*, p. 141.

¹⁸Jung, *Memories, Dreams, Reflections*, p. 338.

¹⁹*Ibid.*, p. 340.

²⁰*Ibid.*, pp. 152–153.

²¹Jung, *Collected Works*, XI, p. 337.

²²Freud, *The Future of an Illusion*, p. 89.

²³Jung, *Collected Works*, XI, p. 469.

²⁴Jung, *Letters*, Vol. II, p. 630.

Chapter 13. Groups: Harmful or Helpful?

¹Jung, *Memories, Dreams, Reflections*, p. 93.

²*Ibid.*, p. 55.

³*Ibid.*, p. 75.

⁴Jung, *Collected Works*, V, p. 70.

⁵Jung, *Collected Works*, XI, pp. 201–296.

⁶Jung, *Letters*, Vol. I, p. 402.

⁷Jung, *Collected Works*, X, p. 471.

⁸*Ibid.*, pp. 275–276.

⁹*Ibid.*, p. 265.

10 Jung, *Collected Works*, XVIII, p. 725.

11 Jung, *Collected Works*, X, p. 258.

12 *Ibid.*, p. 280.

13 Jung, *Collected Works*, XVIII, p. 739.

14 Jung, *Collected Works*, X, p. 257.

15 *Ibid.*, p. 304.

16 Jung, *Collected Works*, XI, p. 331.

17 Jung, *Memories, Dreams, Reflections*, p. 134.

18 See, for example, Peter Berger's argument in *A Rumor of Angels* (Garden City, NY: Doubleday & Company, 1969).

19 Jung, *Letters*, Vol. I, p. 508.

20 Edward Whitmont, "Group Therapy and Analytical Psychology," *The Journal of Analytical Psychology*, Vol. 9, No. 1, January, 1964 (London: Tavistock Publications, 1964), p. 1.

21 William Temple, *Nature, Man and God* (London: Macmillan & Co., 1964), p. 315, note 2.

22 *Ibid.*, p. 322.

23 William Temple, *Readings in St. John's Gospel* (London: Macmillan & Co., 1945), pp. 91–92.

24 Jung, *Collected Works*, XI, p. 301.

25 Irene de Castillejo, *Knowing Woman* (New York: G. P. Putnam's Sons, for the C. G. Jung Foundation for Analytical Psychology, 1973), p. 12. See also Martin Buber, *I and Thou*, 2d ed, trans. Ronald Gregor Smith (New York: Charles Scribner's Sons, 1958).

Chapter 14. Evil as the "Dark Side" of God

1 Jung, *Collected Works*, XI, pp. 357–358.

2 Jung, *Memories, Dreams, Reflections*, pp. 36–41.

3 Jung, *Collected Works*, XI, p. 358.

4 Archibald MacLeish, *J.B.* (Boston: Houghton Mifflin Company, The Riverside Press, 1956), p. 11.

5 See Jung's "A Psychological Approach to the Dogma of the Trinity," *Collected Works*, XI, pp. 107–200. See also Edward Edinger's conclusion: "The trinity archetype seems to symbolize individuation as a process, while the quaternity symbolizes its goal or completed state." *Ego and Archetype* (New York: G. P. Putnam's Sons, for the C. G. Jung Foundation for Analytical Psychology, 1972), p. 193.

6 Jung, *Answer to Job, Collected Works*, XI, p. 463. In a footnote to this passage, Jung commented, "Owing to the undervaluation of the psyche

that everywhere prevails, every attempt at adequate psychological understanding is immediately suspected of psychologism." He added that if, for example, in physics, one sought to explain the nature of light, no one expected that as a result there would be no light. But, on the other hand, in the case of psychology everyone believed that what it explained was explained away.

⁷*Ibid.*, p. 465. See also Erich Neumann's essay, "A Note on Marc Chagall," in *Art and the Creative Unconscious*, trans. Ralph Manheim, Bollingen Series LXI (New York: Pantheon Books, 1959), in which he discusses the reappearance of the missing feminine in Judaism.

⁸This suggestion was made in an address to the C. G. Jung Society of Colorado in May, 1976, by Ann De Vore.

⁹William James, *The Varieties of Religious Experience*, p. 417.

¹⁰Paul Tillich, "Reply to Interpretation and Criticism," in Kegley and Bretall, *The Theology of Paul Tillich*, p. 340. See also: Tillich, *Systematic Theology*, Vol. I (Chicago: The University of Chicago Press, 1951), p. 270.

¹¹See, for example, Tillich's discussion of "Reopening the Trinitarian Problem" in his *Systematic Theology*, Vol. III, p. 294.

¹²Jung, *Memories, Dreams, Reflections*, pp. 52–53.

¹³Jung, *Collected Works*, XVIII, p. 715.

¹⁴*Ibid.*, p. 728.

¹⁵Jung, *Collected Works*, XI, p. 331.

Chapter 15. Evil and the Resurrection Symbol

¹Martin Buber, *I and Thou*, p. 118.

²William James, *The Varieties of Religious Experience*, p. 509.

³Paul Tillich, *Systematic Theology*, Vol. III, p. 422.

⁴See Norman Pittenger's presentation of process theology in *Unbounded Love: God and Man in Process;* A Crossroad Book (New York: The Seabury Press, 1976).

⁵Langdon Gilkey, *Maker of Heaven and Earth;* Anchor Books (Garden City, NY: Doubleday & Company, 1965), p. 358n.

⁶Jung, *Memories, Dreams, Reflections*, p. 353.

⁷Jung, *Collected Works*, XI, p. 345.

⁸Esther Harding, "Jung's Contribution to Religious Symbolism," *Three Papers*, p. 30.

⁹Victor White, O.P., *God and the Unconscious;* Meridian Books (Cleve-

land and New York: The World Publishing Company, 1961), pp. 188–
203.

[10] Tillich, *Systematic Theology*, Vol. I, p. 260.

[11] Gustaf Aulen, *Christus Victor*, trans. A. G. Hebert (New York: Macmillan, 1931).

[12] Jung, *Collected Works*, XVIII, p. 696.

[13] Jung, *Collected Works*, IX (I), pp. 113–115.

[14] Jung, *Collected Works*, XI, p. 183, footnote 4.

Chapter 16. The Holy Spirit and the New Age

[1] Jung, *Collected Works*, XIV, p. 318, footnote 244.

[2] Jung, *Collected Works*, X, p. 279.

[3] See Jung's *Aion, Collected Works*, IX (II), and "A Psychological Approach to the Dogma of the Trinity," *Collected Works*, XI, pp. 107–200.

[4] Jung, *Collected Works*, XVIII, p. 735.

[5] *Ibid.*, p. 736.

[6] *Ibid.*

[7] William Temple, *Readings in St. John's Gospel* (London: Macmillan & Co., 1945), pp. 91–92.

[8] Jung, *Collected Works*, VIII, pp. 417–519.

[9] Jung, *Letters*, Vol. II, p. 435.

[10] *Ibid.*, p. 436.